BARON GUZMAN

SIMPLE CROCKPOT

RECIPES FOR BEGINNERS

Our team consists of:

Author - Baron Guzman
Recipe Tester - Emma Davis
Photographer - Lucas Thompson
Editor - Megan Parker
Graphic Designer - Ryan Foster
Legal Consultant - Sophia Mitchell

Thank you for choosing us.

CONTENTS

CONTENTS

14	Classic Overnight Oats
17	Cinnamon Roll Casserole
19	Nourishing Breakfast Casserole
21	Banana Nut Bread Pudding
22	Classic Overnight Oats
25	Vegetable Beef Stew
27	Creamy Potato Soup
29	Classic Minestrone Soup
30	Nourishing Slow
30	Cooker Chili
31	Suggested Toppings
32	Honey Garlic Chicken
35	BBQ Pulled Pork
37	Easy Beef Pot Roast
39	Slow Cooker Lasagna
41	Vegetable Curry
42	Cheesy Mashed Potatoes
45	Crock Pot Mac & Cheese
47	Creamed Corn
49	Garlic Parmesan Green Beans
51	Slow Cooker Stuffing
52	Lentil Soup
55	Sweet Potato & Chickpea Curry
57	Black Bean Enchiladas
59	Vegan Quinoa Chili
61	Stuffed Bell Peppers
62	Chicken and Rice Casserole
65	Sausage and Peppers
67	Slow Cooker Jambalaya
69	Beef Stroganoff
71	Cajun Shrimp Boil
72	Chocolate Lava Cake
75	Crock Pot Apple Crisp
77	Peach Cobbler
79	Bread Pudding
81	Rice Pudding
82	Buffalo Chicken Dip
85	Spinach & Artichoke Dip
87	Crock Pot Meatballs
89	Nacho Cheese Dip
91	Slow Cooker Chex Mix
92	Essential Tips for Optimal Use
94	Creative Uses
95	Adapting Traditional Recipes

DISCLAIMER

The recipes and advice in *Simple Crockpot Recipes for Beginners* are provided only for general information and educational purposes. While every effort has been made to ensure the accuracy of the information provided, the author assumes no responsibility for errors or omissions. All content is based on the author's research, personal knowledge, and experience at the time of writing.

The reader acknowledges that cooking and meal preparation can involve inherent risks. The author and publisher are not liable for any loss, injury, or damage incurred due to following the recipes or advice contained in this book. Individual results may vary, and the reader is encouraged to modify recipes to suit personal tastes and dietary needs.

Readers should seek advice from medical professionals before starting any new dietary regimen, especially if they have underlying health conditions, food allergies, or specific dietary requirements. The information and recipes in this book are not intended to replace professional advice or treatment from a qualified healthcare provider.

All product and company names mentioned in this book are trademarks or registered trademarks of their respective holders. Using these names does not imply endorsement or affiliation with the trademark holders.

1. WELCOME TO CROCK POT COOKING!

What is a Crock Pot?

1. A Crock Pot, also known as a slow cooker, is a countertop electrical appliance used to simmer food at low temperatures over a long time. Unlike traditional cooking methods that use high heat for short periods, the Crock Pot simmers food, resulting in tender, flavorful dishes with minimal effort. It comprises a removable ceramic or stoneware insert, a heating base, and a lid. The device's simplicity makes it ideal for "set it and forget it" meals, which you can cook while at work, running errands, or simply relaxing.

Why Crock Pot Cooking is Perfect for Beginners

If you're starting in the kitchen, the Crock Pot is one of the most beginner-friendly appliances you can use.

Here's why:

1. **Easy to use**: With just a few basic settings (low, high, warm), anyone can master slow cooking.
2. **Minimal supervision:** Once the ingredients are added and the Crock Pot is turned on, there's no need to watch over it like you would on a stovetop or in the oven.
3. **Foolproof recipes:** Because the Crock Pot uses low heat over extended periods, there's less risk of burning or overcooking food, making it forgiving for beginners.
4. **One-pot meals:** This single appliance can cook entire meals, making clean-up quick and easy.

Benefits of Slow Cooking: Convenience, Flavor, Nutrition

1. **Convenience**: Crock Pot meals are great for busy lifestyles. Chop the ingredients, place them in the pot, and let the slow cooker work magic. You can go about your day knowing that a delicious meal will be waiting when you're ready to eat.
2. **Flavor:** Slow cooking allows the flavors to develop gradually, making dishes like soups, stews, and roasts extra savory and rich. The long cooking process helps break down tough cuts of meat, turning them tender and juicy.
3. **Nutrition:** Crock Pots use low heat and retain moisture, helping preserve nutrients in your ingredients. You can create healthy, well-balanced meals that are highly flavorful without requiring processed ingredients or heavy oils.

How to Use This Cookbook for Your Culinary Journey

1. This cookbook is designed with beginners in mind, offering simple, step-by-step instructions for each recipe. Here's how to make the most of it:
2. **Start simple:** Start with the easiest recipes, which require just a few ingredients. These are perfect for building your confidence in the kitchen.
3. **Explore different meal categories:** From breakfasts to desserts, this book covers a wide range of dishes. Don't be afraid to try something new and broaden your cooking repertoire.
4. **Follow the tips and tricks:** Throughout the book, you'll find helpful tips to make cooking effortless. These include time-saving suggestions, storage ideas, and advice on how to get the most out of your Crock Pot.
5. **Have fun:** Cooking should be enjoyable! Experiment with flavors, try new recipes and feel empowered as you see how easy and delicious Crock Pot meals can be.

1. Lid

2. tempered glass

3. Removable Insert (Crock/ Stoneware Pot)

3. The insert

4. heating element

4. Heating Base

4. Control Panel

PARTS OF A CROCK POT (EXPLAINED)

Understanding the essential components of your Crock Pot will help you use it effectively.

Here are the vital parts:

1. **Removable Insert (Crock/Stoneware Pot):** This is the ceramic or stoneware pot where you place all your ingredients. It' removable for easy cleaning and can sometimes be used directly for serving.
2. **Lid**: The lid is usually made of tempered glass, allowing you to monitor cooking without lifting it. Keeping the lid on whil cooking is crucial for retaining heat and moisture.
3. **Heating Base**: The outer shell houses the heating element. It controls the temperature settings and evenly distributes hea to the insert.
4. **Control Panel:** Depending on the model, this may be a simple dial with low, high, and warm settings or an advanced digita interface with timers and programmable options.

How to Properly Use and Care for Your Crock Pot

To get the most out of your Crock Pot, it's essential to use and maintain it properly:

1. **Preheat (optional)**: While not always necessary, preheating your Crock Pot for about 10-15 minutes before adding ingredients can speed up the cooking process, especially when you're short on time.
2. **Layering Ingredients**: Denser ingredients (like root vegetables and meats) should go at the bottom of the pot, closer to the heat, while lighter ingredients (like leafy greens) should go on top. This ensures even cooking.
3. **Fill Level:** For best results, fill your Crock Pot about halfway to two-thirds full. Overfilling can cause uneven cooking, while underfilling may dry your dish.
4. **Cleaning**: After each use, allow the Crock Pot to cool before cleaning. The removable insert can be washed with warm, soapy water or placed in the dishwasher. The heating base should never be submerged; clean it with a damp cloth. Always ensure that the lid and the insert are fully dry before storing.
5. **Storage:** Store your Crock Pot in a dry place, and avoid placing heavy items on top of it, especially the lid, which can crack.
6. **Essential Cooking Tips:** Timing, Temperature Settings, and Adjusting Recipes
7. **Timing**: Crock Pot cooking typically requires extended cooking times. Recipes generally provide a time range for cooking on low or high heat.
8. **The low setting (about 200°F/93°C)** is best for dishes that need to cook for 6-8 hours or longer. It's ideal for braising meats and creating deeply flavorful stews.
9. **High setting (about 300°F/149°C)**: Use this setting when you need a dish ready in 4-6 hours. It works well for recipes that can handle quicker cooking, like soups and side dishes.
10. **Warm setting:** This is for keeping food warm after cooking, not for cooking food. Avoid leaving food on warm for more than 4 hours.
11. **Adjusting Recipes**: Most traditional recipes can be adapted for the Crock Pot. A general rule is to reduce the liquid content slightly (since the slow cooker retains moisture) and adjust the cooking time. For example, if a stovetop recipe calls for 30 minutes of simmering, that would translate to roughly 4-6 hours on low in a Crock Pot.

Safety Tips for Slow Cooking

1. **Preheat Meat:** While you don't always need to pre-cook ingredients, it's a good idea to brown meats before adding them to the Crock Pot. This enhances flavor and ensures food safety, mainly when using beef, pork, or poultry cuts.
2. **Avoid Overfilling**: As mentioned, keep the Crock Pot filled between half and two-thirds full. Overfilling can cause food to cook unevenly and may result in spillage.
3. **Do Not Lift the Lid During Cooking**: Each time you lift the lid, heat escapes, and you lose cooking time. Avoid lifting the lid unless necessary, especially in the first half of the cooking process.
4. **Refrigerate Leftovers Properly**: After cooking, store leftovers in shallow containers and refrigerate them within 2 hours to prevent bacteria growth.
5. **Use Safe Cooking Temperatures**: To ensure food safety, meats should reach an internal temperature of at least 165°F (74°C). If needed, check with a food thermometer.

ESSENTIAL INGREDIENTS FOR EASY CROCK POT COOKING

Stocking your pantry with essential ingredients will help you prepare Crock Pot meals effortlessly. These staples are versatile, shelf-stable, and ideal for various recipes.

Canned Goods:

Beans: Black beans, kidney beans, chickpeas, and cannellini beans are perfect for soups, stews, and chili.

Tomatoes: Diced, crushed, and whole canned tomatoes are great for sauces, soups, and stews.

Broths/Stocks: Chicken, beef, or vegetable broth adds flavor and moisture to Crock Pot dishes.

Coconut Milk: Adds creaminess and flavor to curries and other dishes.

Grains and Pasta:

Rice: Brown rice, basmati, or jasmine rice for hearty, one-pot meals.

Pasta: Short pasta like penne or macaroni works best in Crock Pot dishes that require less liquid absorption.

Quinoa: A protein-packed grain that cooks well in soups and stews.

Dry Goods:

Lentils: Red or green lentils are great for thickening soups and stews.

Potatoes: Yukon gold, red potatoes, or sweet potatoes hold up well in slow cooking.

Oats: Steel-cut oats for breakfast dishes like overnight oatmeal.

Proteins:

Chicken: Boneless, skinless chicken breasts or thighs are easy to cook and versatile.

Beef: Slow-cooker favorites include Chuck roast, stew, or ground beef.

Pork: Pork shoulder or tenderloin is perfect for pulled pork or stews.

Recommended Herbs, Spices, and Flavor Boosters

Spices and herbs add depth to your slow-cooked meals. Keep a selection of these essentials on hand to enhance the flavors of your dishes.

Herbs:

- Bay Leaves: Great for soups, stews, and braises.
- Thyme: Adds a savory, earthy note to meats and vegetables.
- Rosemary: Pairs well with poultry, pork, and lamb.
- Parsley: Fresh or dried parsley adds color and brightness to soups and stews.
- Basil and Oregano: Both are perfect for Italian-inspired dishes like lasagna or tomato-based sauces.

Spices:

- Garlic Powder and Onion Powder: Simple yet essential for flavoring almost any dish.
- Paprika: Adds warmth and smokiness, especially in stews, chili, and meat dishes.
- Cumin: Great for adding a rich, earthy flavor to beans, soups, and Mexican-inspired dishes.
- Curry Powder: For a burst of flavor in Indian or Asian dishes.
- Chili Powder: A must-have for chili, tacos, and spicy dishes.
- Ground Cinnamon and Nutmeg: Perfect for sweet recipes like desserts or spiced fall dishes.

Flavor Boosters:

- Soy Sauce: Adds umami and depth to Asian-inspired dishes.
- Worcestershire Sauce: Great for boosting the savory flavor in meat dishes and gravies.
- Balsamic Vinegar: Adds tang and sweetness to sauces and meat-based dishes.
- Hot Sauce: For a spicy kick in soups, stews, and dips.
- Brown Sugar/Honey/Maple Syrup: Adds a touch of sweetness to BBQ dishes, glazes, or desserts.
- Lemon Juice: This is for brightness and acidity to balance heavy flavors.

Substitutions and Shopping on a Budget

Cooking with a Crock Pot doesn't need to break the bank. Here are some money-saving tips and simple ingredient substitutions to help you stick to your budget while creating delicious meals.

Protein Substitutions:

1. Beans/Lentils for Meat: Substitute some or all of the meat in a recipe with beans or lentils for a budget-friendly, protein-packed alternative. They absorb flavors well in slow cooking.
2. Ground Turkey or Chicken for Beef: These options are often cheaper and as versatile in soups, stews, and casseroles.
3. Bone-in Meats: Opt for bone-in cuts of chicken (like thighs or drumsticks) or pork. These are more affordable, and the bones add flavor.

Vegetable Substitutions:

4. Frozen Vegetables: Use frozen veggies in place of fresh ones. They're more affordable and just as nutritious. Frozen peas, spinach, and corn work great in many Crock Pot dishes.
5. Cabbage, Carrots, and Root Vegetables are inexpensive, hearty vegetables that can stretch a meal and hold up well in slow cooking.

Herb and Spice Substitutions:

6. Fresh vs. Dried Herbs: Dried herbs are more budget-friendly and have a longer shelf life. Generally, one teaspoon of dried herbs is used for every tablespoon of fresh herbs called for in a recipe.
7. Homemade Seasoning Blends: Instead of buying pre-mixed seasoning packets (expensive and full of additives), make your blends with pantry spices like garlic powder, cumin, paprika, and salt.

Budget-Friendly Tips:

1. Bulk Purchases: Buy bulk pantry staples like rice, beans, and spices to save money over time.
2. Sales and Freezer Stocking: Purchase meats and vegetables when on sale and freeze them for future use. This is especially helpful for stocking up on expensive items like chicken breasts or beef roasts.
3. Make Larger Batches: Cook larger batches and freeze the leftovers for future meals. This saves money on groceries and reduces food waste.

CLASSIC OVERNIGHT OATS

INSTRUCTIONS

1. Prepare the Slow Cooker: Lightly grease the inside of your slow cooker with a small amount of oil or non-stick spray to prevent the oats from sticking. This will also make cleanup easier.

2. Add Ingredients: Into the slow cooker, combine the rolled oats, almond milk (or milk of choice), chia seeds (if using), maple syrup, vanilla extract, cinnamon, and salt. Stir well to ensure that all ingredients are evenly distributed.

3. Customize the Mix: If you'd like, add any optional ingredients like flaxseed, shredded coconut, or dried fruit for extra texture, flavor, and nutrition.

4. Set and Cook: Cover the slow cooker with the lid and cook on low for 6-8 hours. The longer the oats cook, the creamier they'll become. If using a programmable slow cooker, set it to switch to the warm setting once the cooking time is complete. This will keep the oats ready for breakfast without overcooking.

5. Check Consistency: In the morning, give the oats a good stir to check the consistency. If they seem too thick, you can add a little more milk to achieve the desired texture. Stir in well.

6. Serve: Ladle the warm oats into bowls and customize with your choice of toppings like fresh fruit, nuts, seeds, nut butter, or a drizzle of maple syrup.

6 PERSON   **6-8 HOURS**   **5 MINUTES**

INGREDIENTS

- 2 cups old-fashioned rolled oats
- 4 cups unsweetened almond milk (or any milk of choice, such as dairy, oat, or coconut milk)
- 2 tablespoons chia seeds (optional, for added fiber and texture)
- 2 tablespoons maple syrup (or honey, optional for sweetness)
- 1 teaspoon vanilla extract
- 1 teaspoon ground cinnamon
- 1/4 teaspoon salt
- 1/4 cup ground flaxseed (optional, for added omega-3s and fiber)
- 1/4 cup unsweetened shredded coconut (optional for added texture and flavor)
- 1/4 cup dried cranberries or raisins (optional for a touch of natural sweetness)

OPTIONAL TOPPINGS OR GARNISHES

- Fresh fruit (sliced bananas, berries, or apples)
- Nuts and seeds (walnuts, almonds, sunflower seeds)
- Nut butter (peanut butter, almond butter)
- Extra maple syrup or honey

TIPS FOR SUCCESS

Time-saving Prep: To make mornings easier, prepare the dry ingredients (oats, chia seeds, cinnamon, salt) in advance. Combine them in a jar, and when ready, pour them into the slow cooker with your milk and other wet ingredients.

Nutritional Boost: Adding chia seeds and flaxseed provides additional fiber, omega-3 fatty acids, and antioxidants, making this a highly nutritious breakfast option.

Dietary Preferences: This recipe is naturally dairy-free and vegan if you use plant-based milk. You can adjust the sweetness to your preference or leave out sweeteners entirely.

- CALORIES: 180
- PROTEIN: 6G
- CARBOHYDRATES: 30G
- FIBER: 6G
- SUGAR: 5G - FAT: 4G
- SATURATED FAT: 0.5G
- CHOLESTEROL: 0MG
- SODIUM: 150MG
- POTASSIUM: 220MG

THIS SLOW-COOKED CLASSIC OVERNIGHT OATS RECIPE IS PER-FECT FOR THOSE SEEKING A HEALTHY, EASY, AND VERSATILE BREAKFAST. WITH MINIMAL PREP AND THE ABILITY TO COOK WHILE YOU SLEEP, IT'S A TIME-SAVING SOLUTION THAT ENSURES YOU WAKE UP TO A NOURISHING AND HEARTY MEAL. THE OATS CAN BE STORED IN THE REFRIGERATOR FOR UP TO 4 DAYS, MAK-ING IT AN EXCELLENT OPTION FOR MEAL PREP.

6-8 PERSON   **2-3 HOURS**   **10 MINUTES**

INSTRUCTIONS

1. Prepare the Slow Cooker: - Grease the inside of your slow cooker with the butter or non-stick spray to prevent sticking and make cleanup easier.

2. Prepare the Cinnamon Rolls: - Open both cans of refrigerated cinnamon rolls. Set the icing packets aside (you will use these later). - Cut each cinnamon roll into quarters and set them aside.

3. Layer the Cinnamon Rolls: - Place the quartered cinnamon rolls evenly at the bottom of the slow cooker. - If desired, sprinkle the chopped pecans and raisins over the cinnamon rolls to add extra flavor and texture.

4. Prepare the Egg Mixture: - In a mixing bowl, whisk together the eggs, heavy cream, vanilla extract, cinnamon, and nutmeg until fully combined. - If using maple syrup, add it to the mixture for an extra touch of sweetness.

5. Pour Over the Cinnamon Rolls: - Pour the egg mixture evenly over the cinnamon rolls in the slow cooker, ensuring that the liquid covers all the pieces for even cooking.

6. Cook the Casserole: - Cover the slow cooker with the lid and cook on low for 2-3 hours, or until the cinnamon rolls are cooked through and the egg mixture is set. - To avoid overcooking, check for doneness at the 2-hour mark. The cinnamon rolls should be soft and springy in the center.

7. Finish with Icing: - Once fully cooked, drizzle the icing from the reserved cinnamon roll packets over the top of the casserole while it's still warm.

8. Serve: - Slice and serve warm. You can add additional toppings such as more maple syrup, whipped cream, or fresh fruit for an extra treat.

INGREDIENTS

- 2 cans (12.4 oz each) refrigerated cinnamon rolls (with icing)
- 4 large eggs
- 1/2 cup heavy cream (or half-and-half for a lighter option)
- 1 tablespoon vanilla extract
- 1 teaspoon ground cinnamon
- 1/4 teaspoon ground nutmeg (optional, for added flavor)
- 1/2 cup maple syrup (optional, for extra sweetness)
- 1/4 cup chopped pecans (optional, for crunch and added nutrition)
- 1/4 cup raisins (optional, for a fruity twist)
- 1 tablespoon unsalted butter, for greasing the slow cooker

NUTRITIONAL

- Calories: 380
- Protein: 7g
- Carbohydrates: 54g
- Fiber: 1g
- Sugar: 23g
- Fat: 15g
- Saturated Fat: 8g
- Cholesterol: 130mg
- Sodium: 500mg
- Potassium: 100mg

TIPS FOR SUCCESS

- Customizable Additions: Feel free to experiment with additional toppings such as chopped apples or sliced bananas, or swap the pecans for walnuts or almonds.
- Dairy-Free Option: To make this recipe dairy-free, substitute heavy cream with coconut milk and use a non-dairy icing or glaze.
- Meal Prep: This casserole can be stored in the fridge for up to 3 days. Reheat individual portions in the microwave for a quick, indulgent breakfast or snack.

CROCK POT CINNAMON
ROLL CASSEROLE

- CUSTOMIZABLE VEG-
GIES: FEEL FREE TO
SWAP THE BELL PEP-
PERS FOR MUSHROOMS,
ZUCCHINI, OR OTHER
FAVORITE VEGETABLES
TO SUIT YOUR TASTE.
SPINACH ADDS A NUTRI-
ENT BOOST BUT CAN BE
OMITTED OR REPLACED
WITH KALE OR ARUGU-
LA.
- MAKE IT DAIRY-
FREE: SUBSTITUTE THE
CHEESE WITH A PLANT-
BASED OPTION AND
USE NON-DAIRY MILK
LIKE ALMOND OR CO-
CONUT MILK FOR A
LACTOSE-FREE ALTER-
NATIVE.
- MEAL PREP: THIS CAS-
SEROLE CAN BE STORED
IN THE REFRIGERATOR
FOR UP TO 4 DAYS. IT
REHEATS WELL, MAKING
IT AN IDEAL MEAL-PREP
OPTION FOR BREAK-
FAST, LUNCH, OR DIN-
NER.

THIS SLOW-COOKER BREAKFAST CASSE-ROLE IS PACKED WITH PROTEIN FROM EGGS AND SAUSAGE, FIBER FROM VEGETABLES, AND HEALTHY FATS. IT'S A NUTRIENT-DENSE MEAL THAT PROVIDES ENERGY TO START THE DAY OR FUELS A BAL-ANCED MEAL AT ANY TIME. SLOW COOKING ENHANCES THE FLA-VORS WHILE WAKING YOU TO A READY-MADE MEAL, PERFECT FOR BUSY MORNINGS OR MEAL-PREPPING FOR THE WEEK.

NOURISHING BREAKFAST CASSEROLE

| 6-8 PERSON | 6-8 HOURS | 15 MINUTES |

INSTRUCTIONS

1. Prepare the Sausage and Veggies: - In a skillet, cook the breakfast sausage over medium heat, breaking it into crumbles. Cook until browned and cooked through, about 5-7 minutes. If using vegetarian sausage, follow the package instructions. - Remove the sausage and set aside. In the same skillet, sauté the diced onion and bell peppers until they are softened, about 3-4 minutes.

2. Assemble the Slow Cooker: - Lightly grease the inside of your slow cooker with non-stick spray or a small amount of oil. - Layer the ingredients: Start with half of the frozen hash browns, followed by half of the sausage, sautéed vegetables, and shredded cheese. Repeat this layering process with the remaining ingredients, finishing with the cheese.

3. Whisk the Eggs: - In a large mixing bowl, whisk together the eggs, milk, garlic powder, salt, black pepper, and smoked paprika (if using) until fully combined.

4. Pour Over the Ingredients: - Slowly pour the egg mixture evenly over the layered ingredients in the slow cooker, ensuring everything is well-covered. If you add spinach, gently mix it into the egg mixture for even distribution.

5. Cook the Casserole: - Cover the slow cooker with the lid and cook on low for 6-8 hours. The casserole is done when the eggs are fully set in the center, and a knife inserted comes out clean. - For a quicker option, you can cook on high for 3-4 hours, though low and slow yields a more tender result.

6. Serve: - Once fully cooked, turn the slow cooker to warm to keep the casserole ready to serve. Slice into portions and serve with your choice of toppings, such as avocado, green onions, salsa, or hot sauce for extra flavor.

INGREDIENTS

- 1 pound breakfast sausage (pork, turkey, or vegetarian sausage)
- 1 medium onion, diced
- 1 red bell pepper, diced
- 1 green bell pepper, diced
- 2 cups fresh spinach (optional for added nutrition)
- 1 ½ cups shredded cheddar cheese (or dairy-free alternative)
- 12 large eggs
- ½ cup milk (dairy or plant-based milk such as almond or oat milk)
- 4 cups frozen hash browns (shredded or cubed)
- 1 teaspoon garlic powder
- 1 teaspoon salt
- ½ teaspoon black pepper
- ½ teaspoon smoked paprika (optional for added flavor)
- Optional toppings: diced avocado, chopped green onions, salsa, hot sauce

NUTRITIONAL

- Calories: 320
- Protein: 18g
- Carbohydrates: 18g
- Fiber: 3g
- Sugar: 2g
- Fat: 20g
- Saturated Fat: 8g
- Cholesterol: 280mg
- Sodium: 720mg
- Potassium: 580mg

INSTRUCTIONS

1. Prepare the Bread: - Use day-old bread for the best texture. Cut the bread into 1-inch cubes and set them aside in a large bowl.
2. Grease the Slow Cooker: - Grease the inside of your slow cooker with butter or non-stick spray to prevent sticking and make cleanup easier.
3. Prepare the Wet Ingredients: - In a mixing bowl, whisk together the mashed bananas, eggs, milk, heavy cream, brown sugar, vanilla extract, cinnamon, nutmeg (if using), and salt until smooth.
4. Assemble the Bread Pudding: - Add the cubed bread and chopped walnuts (and any optional additions like raisins or chocolate chips) to the banana mixture. Gently toss everything together until the bread cubes are evenly coated with the wet mixture.
5. Transfer to Slow Cooker: - Pour the bread mixture into the greased slow cooker. Spread it out evenly, pressing down slightly to ensure all the bread is submerged in the liquid.
6. Cook the Bread Pudding: - Cover the slow cooker with the lid and cook on low for 2-3 hours. The bread pudding is done when it is set in the center and a knife inserted comes out mostly clean. Cooking time may vary depending on the slow cooker model, so check at the 2-hour mark.
7. Serve: - Once cooked, turn off the slow cooker and let the bread pudding rest for 10-15 minutes before serving. This allows it to firm up slightly and cool down.
8. Top and Enjoy: - Serve warm with your choice of toppings like sliced bananas, whipped cream, or a drizzle of maple syrup for extra sweetness.

INGREDIENTS

- 6 cups of cubed bread (day-old French bread, brioche, or whole grain bread for extra fiber)
- 3 ripe bananas, mashed
- 1 cup chopped walnuts (or pecans for a variation)
- 4 large eggs
- 1 ½ cups milk (dairy or plant-based milk like almond, oat, or coconut)
- ½ cup heavy cream (or use more milk for a lighter option)
- ½ cup brown sugar
- 1 tablespoon vanilla extract
- 1 teaspoon ground cinnamon
- ¼ teaspoon ground nutmeg (optional, for added warmth)
- Pinch of salt
- 2 tablespoons unsalted butter, for greasing the slow cooker
- Optional additions: ¼ cup raisins or chocolate chips for extra flavor

TOPPINGS OR GARNISHES

- Sliced bananas
- Whipped cream or a dollop of Greek yogurt
- Drizzle of maple syrup or honey
- Chopped nuts for crunch

TIPS FOR SUCCESS

Bread Choice: Day-old or slightly stale bread works best for bread pudding, as it absorbs the liquid more effectively without becoming mushy. Whole-grain bread adds extra fiber and nutrition to the dish.
- Dairy-Free Option: For a dairy-free version, use almond or coconut milk and skip the heavy cream or substitute with a plant-based cream alternative.
- Banana Flavor Boost: For a more robust banana flavor, use extra-ripe bananas, which add natural sweetness and fragrance.
- Make Ahead: This recipe can be assembled the night before and stored in the refrigerator. In the morning, transfer to the slow cooker and start cooking.

NUTRITIONAL

- Calories: 380
- Protein: 7g
- Carbohydrates: 54g
- Fiber: 1g
- Sugar: 23g
- Fat: 15g
- Saturated Fat: 8g
- Cholesterol: 130mg
- Sodium: 500mg
- Potassium: 100mg

BANANA NUT BREAD
PUDDING

CLASSIC OVERNIGHT OATS

6 PERSON

6-8 HOURS

15 MINUTES

INSTRUCTIONS

1. Prepare Ingredients:

   Dice the onion, slice the carrots, and chop the celery. Mince the garlic.

   If using fresh thyme, strip the leaves from the stems.

2. Sauté Vegetables (Optional but Recommended):

   Heat olive oil in a skillet over medium heat. Add onions, carrots, and celery. Sauté for about 5 minutes until softened.

   Add minced garlic and cook for another 1-2 minutes until fragrant. This step enhances the soup's flavor but can be skipped if you're short on time.

3. Assemble the Soup:

   Transfer the sautéed vegetables (or raw vegetables if you skipped the sautéing) to the slow cooker.

   Add the chicken breasts, chicken broth, bay leaf, thyme, salt, and black pepper to the slow cooker.

4. Cook:

   Cover and cook on low for 6-8 hours or high for 3-4 hours.

   About 30 minutes before serving, shred the chicken breasts with two forks directly in the slow cooker.

   Add the uncooked egg noodles and stir. Continue cooking until noodles are tender.

5. Optional Additions:

   If using frozen peas, add them in the last 30 minutes of cooking.

6. Adjust Seasoning:

   Taste the soup and adjust salt and pepper if needed. Remove the bay leaf before serving.

7. Serve:

   Ladle the soup into bowls and garnish with chopped fresh parsley if desired.

INGREDIENTS

Boneless, skinless chicken breasts: 1 lb (about 2 cups cooked and shredded)
Carrots: 2 medium, peeled and sliced
Celery stalks: 2, chopped
Onion: 1 medium, diced
Garlic cloves: 3, minced
Chicken broth: 6 cups (low-sodium recommended)
Egg noodles: 2 cups (uncooked)
Bay leaf: 1
Thyme: 1 teaspoon (dried) or 1 tablespoon (fresh)
Salt: 1 teaspoon (adjust to taste)
Black pepper: ½ teaspoon (adjust to taste)
Olive oil: 1 tablespoon (for sautéing vegetables)
Optional additions:
Frozen peas: 1 cup (added in the last 30 minutes of cooking)
Chopped fresh parsley: 2 tablespoons (for garnish)

HEALTH BENEFITS AND CONVENIENCE

Convenience: The slow cooker makes it easy to prepare this soup with minimal hands-on time. Set it up in the morning, and come home to a warm, comforting meal.
Nourishing: This soup is rich in lean protein from chicken, with a good balance of vegetables and carbohydrates from the noodles.
Versatile: Can be customized with additional vegetables or herbs to suit dietary preferences or nutritional needs.

TOPPINGS AND GARNISHES

Fresh parsley: Adds a burst of color and freshness.
Crackers or crusty bread: For a crunchy side.
Grated Parmesan cheese: For added flavor.

ENJOY THIS EASY, HEARTY CHICKEN NOODLE SOUP, PERFECT FOR ANY MEAL AND MADE SIMPLE WITH THE SLOW COOKER!

6 PERSON   **8 HOURS**   **20 MINUTES**

INSTRUCTIONS

1. Brown the Beef (Optional but recommended):
    Heat 2 tablespoons of olive oil in a large skillet over medium-high heat. Season the beef cubes with salt and pepper, then brown them in the skillet until all sides are seared (about 4-5 minutes). Transfer the browned beef to your slow cooker.

2. Prepare Vegetables:
    While the beef is browning, chop the carrots, potatoes, onion, celery, and garlic. Add them to the slow cooker along with the green beans and frozen peas.

3. Add the Liquids and Seasoning:
    Pour the beef broth and diced tomatoes (with juice) into the slow cooker. Stir in the tomato paste, Worcestershire sauce, thyme, oregano, smoked paprika (if using), and bay leaf. Season with salt and pepper to taste.

4. Optional Grains:
    If you're adding barley or quinoa, stir them in at this point. These grains will absorb the flavors and thicken the stew as it cooks.

5. Set the Slow Cooker:
    Cover the slow cooker with the lid.
    For low heat: Set the slow cooker to low and cook for 8 hours.
    For high heat: Set it to high and cook for 4-5 hours.

6. Finishing Touches:
    About 30 minutes before the stew is done, check the consistency and seasoning. Add more salt and pepper if necessary. Remove the bay leaf.

7. Serve:
    Once cooked, ladle the stew into bowls and garnish with fresh parsley. Serve with crusty bread or on its own for a hearty meal.

INGREDIENTS

1 lb (450g) beef stew meat, cut into bite-sized cubes
4 medium carrots, peeled and sliced
3 medium potatoes, peeled and diced
1 medium onion, chopped
3 cloves garlic, minced
2 celery stalks, chopped
1 cup green beans, trimmed and cut into 1-inch pieces
1 cup frozen peas
4 cups low-sodium beef broth
1 can (14.5 oz/410g) diced tomatoes, with juice
2 tablespoons tomato paste
1 tablespoon Worcestershire sauce
1 teaspoon dried thyme
1 teaspoon dried oregano
1 teaspoon smoked paprika (optional for extra flavor)
1 bay leaf
Salt and pepper, to taste
2 tablespoons olive oil (for browning meat)
1/4 cup fresh parsley, chopped (for garnish)

OPTIONAL ADDITIONS

-1/2 cup barley or quinoa (for extra fiber and nutrients)
-1 cup mushrooms, sliced
-1 teaspoon cumin or coriander (for extra warmth in flavor)

TOPPINGS OR GARNISHES

-Fresh parsley (chopped)
-Grated Parmesan cheese
-A dollop of sour cream or Greek yogurt for added creaminess
-Croutons for crunch

NUTRITIONAL

- Calories: 380
- Protein: 7g
- Carbohydrates: 54g
- Fiber: 1g
- Sugar: 23g
- Fat: 15g
- Saturated Fat: 8g
- Cholesterol: 130mg
- Sodium: 500mg
- Potassium: 100mg

VEGETABLE BEEF STEW

SLOW COOKING HELPS RETAIN NUTRIENTS IN VEGETABLES
AND PROTEINS WHILE CREATING RICH, DEEP FLAVORS. IT'S
A LOW-MAINTENANCE COOKING METHOD THAT PROMOTES
HEALTHY EATING BY USING LEAN MEATS AND NUTRIENT-DENSE
VEGETABLES. PLUS, IT'S CONVENIENT FOR BUSY SCHEDULES AND
PERFECT FOR BATCH COOKING.

COOKED BACON BITS
SHREDDED CHEDDAR
CHEESE
CHOPPED GREEN ON-
IONS OR CHIVES
FRESH PARSLEY
CROUTONS

THIS CREAMY POTATO SOUP IS NOT ONLY COMFORTING AND DELICIOUS BUT ALSO QUITE CONVENIENT. THE SLOW COOKER ALLOWS FOR HANDS-OFF PREPARATION, MAKING IT IDEAL FOR BUSY DAYS. POTATOES ARE A GOOD SOURCE OF VITAMINS AND MINERALS, INCLUDING POTASSIUM, WHICH HELPS WITH HEART HEALTH AND MUSCLE FUNCTION. BY USING LOW-SODIUM BROTH AND OPTIONAL DAIRY-FREE ALTERNATIVES, YOU CAN ADJUST THE RECIPE TO MEET VARIOUS DIETARY PREFERENCES AND NEEDS. PLUS, THE SLOW COOKING PROCESS ENHANCES THE FLAVORS AND CREATES A RICH, SATISFYING SOUP THAT'S PERFECT FOR ANY MEAL OF THE DAY.

CREAMY POTATO SOUP

6 PERSON

6-8 HOURS

20 MINUTES

INSTRUCTIONS

1. Prepare Ingredients: Peel and dice the potatoes into small, bite-sized pieces. Dice the onion and mince the garlic. If using, chop the carrots or celery.

2. Sauté Aromatics (Optional): In a skillet over medium heat, melt the butter. Add the diced onion and garlic and sauté until softened and fragrant, about 3-4 minutes. This step adds extra flavor but can be skipped if you prefer a simpler preparation.

3. Combine in Slow Cooker: Place the diced potatoes, sautéed onion and garlic (if used), and any additional vegetables in the slow cooker. Pour in the chicken or vegetable broth, ensuring the vegetables are covered. Season with thyme, rosemary, salt, and pepper.

4. Cook: Set the slow cooker to low and cook for 6-8 hours, or set it to high and cook for 3-4 hours, until the potatoes are tender and easily pierced with a fork.

5. Blend Soup: Once cooked, use an immersion blender to blend the soup until smooth and creamy. Alternatively, carefully transfer batches of the soup to a countertop blender, blend until smooth, and return to the slow cooker.

6. Add Cream and Cheese: Stir in the milk, heavy cream, and shredded cheddar cheese (if using). If the soup is too thick, add a bit more milk to reach your desired consistency. Taste and adjust seasoning with additional salt and pepper if needed.

7. Thicken Soup (Optional): If you prefer a thicker soup, whisk the flour with a bit of cold water to make a slurry. Stir the slurry into the soup and cook on high for an additional 30 minutes until thickened.

8. Serve: Ladle the creamy potato soup into bowls and garnish with optional toppings like cooked bacon bits, chopped green onions, or fresh parsley.

INGREDIENTS

4 large russet potatoes, peeled and diced
1 medium onion, diced
2 cloves garlic, minced
3 cups low-sodium chicken or vegetable broth
1 cup whole milk (or plant-based milk for a dairy-free version)
1 cup heavy cream (or a dairy-free cream alternative)
1 cup shredded cheddar cheese (optional, or use a dairy-free cheese)
2 tablespoons unsalted butter (or olive oil for a dairy-free version)
1 teaspoon dried thyme
1 teaspoon dried rosemary
Salt and pepper, to taste
2 tablespoons all-purpose flour (optional, for thickening)

NUTRITIONAL

Calories: 290 kcal
Protein: 7g
Carbohydrates: 31g
Fat: 15g
Fiber: 3g
Cholesterol: 56mg
Sodium: 640mg
Potassium: 890mg

OPTIONAL ADDITIONS:

1 cup chopped carrots or celery for extra nutrition and texture
1 cup cooked bacon bits for added flavor
1/2 cup chopped green onions or chives for garnish
1/4 cup fresh parsley, chopped for garnish

6 PERSON **6-8 HOURS** **15 MINUTES**

INSTRUCTIONS

1. Prepare Ingredients:
    Chop all vegetables as specified.
2. Sauté Aromatics (Optional but recommended):
    Heat the olive oil in a skillet over medium heat. Add the chopped onion and cook until softened, about 5 minutes.
    Add the minced garlic and cook for an additional minute until fragrant. Transfer to the slow cooker.
3. Add Vegetables and Beans:
    In the slow cooker, combine the sautéed onion and garlic with the carrots, celery, zucchini, bell pepper, and green beans.
4. Add Canned Ingredients and Spices:
    Stir in the diced tomatoes (with juice), kidney beans, chickpeas, vegetable broth, bay leaf, basil, oregano, thyme, salt, and black pepper.
5. Slow Cook:
    Cover and cook on low for 6-8 hours or on high for 4 hours.
6. Add Pasta:
    About 30 minutes before the soup is done, stir in the pasta. If cooking on high, add the pasta about 15 minutes before the soup is finished. Cook until the pasta is tender.
7. Finish:
    If using, stir in chopped spinach or kale during the last 10 minutes of cooking. Add lemon juice if desired for extra flavor.

INGREDIENTS

2 tablespoons olive oil
1 medium onion, chopped
3 cloves garlic, minced
2 medium carrots, diced
2 celery stalks, diced
1 medium zucchini, diced
1 red bell pepper, diced
1 cup green beans, cut into 1-inch pieces
1 (14.5-ounce) can diced tomatoes (with juice)
1 (15-ounce) can kidney beans, drained and rinsed
1 (15-ounce) can chickpeas (garbanzo beans), drained and rinsed
4 cups vegetable broth
1 bay leaf
1 teaspoon dried basil
1 teaspoon dried oregano
1 teaspoon dried thyme
Salt and black pepper, to taste
1 cup small pasta (such as elbow macaroni or ditalini)

OPTIONAL ADDITIONS

1 cup chopped spinach or kale
1 tablespoon lemon juice
(for added brightness)
1/4 cup grated Parmesan cheese
(for serving)

TOPPINGS OR GARNISHES

Fresh Basil or Parsley:
For added freshness.
Croutons or Toasted Bread:
For extra crunch.
Grated Parmesan Cheese:
For a savory, rich flavor.

SERVE

Ladle the soup into bowls. Optionally, sprinkle with grated Parmesan cheese before serving.

NUTRITIONAL

Calories: 210
Protein: 9g
Carbohydrates: 34g
Fat: 5g
Fiber: 8g
Cholesterol: 0mg
Sodium: 700mg
Potassium: 800mg

CLASSIC MINESTRONE SOUP

- NUTRIENT RETENTION: SLOW COOKING HELPS PRESERVE VITAMINS AND MINERALS IN THE VEGETABLES.
FLAVOR DEVELOPMENT: THE EXTENDED COOKING TIME ALLOWS FLAVORS TO MELD TOGETHER, ENHANCING THE TASTE.
CONVENIENCE: SET IT UP IN THE MORNING AND COME HOME TO A HOT, READY MEAL, WHICH IS PERFECT FOR BUSY SCHEDULES.
CUSTOMIZABLE: THIS RECIPE CAN BE ADAPTED TO ACCOMMODATE VARIOUS DIETARY PREFERENCES AND RESTRICTIONS, INCLUDING VEGETARIAN, VEGAN (BY OMITTING CHEESE), AND GLUTEN-FREE (BY USING GLUTEN-FREE PASTA).

NOURISHING SLOW
COOKER CHILI

6 PERSON   **6-8 HOURS**   **15 MINUTES**

OPTIONAL ADDITIONS
1 cup corn kernels (fresh o[r]
frozen[)]
1 medium zucchini, chopped
(for added vegetables[)]
1 tbsp cocoa powder (for [a]
rich depth of flavor[)]
1 tsp maple syrup or honey
(to balance the heat[)]

INSTRUCTIONS

1. Prepare the Ingredients:
   If using ground meat, heat a skillet over medium heat, add olive oil, and brown the meat until fully cooked. Drain any excess fat.
   In the same skillet, sauté the chopped onion, garlic, and bell pepper until softened (about 3-5 minutes). This step is optional but adds depth to the flavor.

2. Assemble in the Slow Cooker:
   Add the cooked meat, sautéed vegetables, beans, diced tomatoes, tomato sauce, broth, and all spices (chili powder, cumin, smoked paprika, oregano, cayenne pepper, salt, and pepper) into the slow cooker.
   Stir well to combine all the ingredients evenly.

3. Cooking Settings:
   For Low Heat: Cover and cook on low for 6-8 hours. This method allows the flavors to meld beautifully.
   For High Heat: Cook on high for 3-4 hours if you're short on time. The chili will still develop great flavor, but the longer, slower cooking method is preferred for deeper taste.

4. Adjust Consistency:
   If the chili is too thick for your preference, you can stir in a little more broth during the last hour of cooking.
   If it's too thin, remove the lid for the last 30 minutes to let the chili reduce slightly.

5. Serve and Garnish:
   Ladle the chili into bowls and serve with your favorite toppings.

INGREDIENTS:

1 lb (450g) lean ground beef (or ground turkey for a lighter option)
1 medium onion, finely chopped
3 cloves garlic, minced
1 bell pepper, chopped (any color)
1 (15 oz) can kidney beans, drained and rinsed
1 (15 oz) can black beans, drained and rinsed
1 (15 oz) can diced tomatoes (with juices)
1 (15 oz) can tomato sauce
1 cup vegetable or beef broth (low sodium)
2 tbsp chili powder
1 tsp cumin
1 tsp smoked paprika
1/2 tsp oregano
1/2 tsp cayenne pepper (optional for extra heat)
Salt and pepper to taste
1 tbsp olive oil (optional for sautéing)

SUGGESTED TOPPINGS

- SOUR CREAM OR GREEK YOGURT (OR A PLANT-BASED ALTERNATIVE)

- SHREDDED CHEESE (CHEDDAR, MONTEREY JACK, OR DAIRY-FREE OPTIONS)

- SLICED AVOCADO

- DICED JALAPEÑOS

- FRESH CILANTRO

- LIME WEDGES

- CRUSHED TORTILLA CHIPS OR CORNBREAD ON THE SIDE

NUTRITIONAL

Calories: 350 kcal
Protein: 24g
Carbohydrates: 35g
Fat: 12g
Fiber: 11g
Cholesterol: 55mg
Sodium: 780mg (varies with broth and canned products)
Potassium: 1050mg

HIGH PROTEIN: WITH BEANS AND LEAN MEAT OR TURKEY, THIS CHILI PROVIDES A HEALTHY DOSE OF PROTEIN.
HIGH FIBER: BEANS AND VEGETABLES ADD FIBER, SUPPORTING DIGESTIVE HEALTH.
LOW FAT OPTION: USE GROUND TURKEY AND OMIT THE OIL FOR A LOWER-FAT VERSION.
VEGETARIAN ADAPTATION: SKIP THE MEAT AND DOUBLE THE BEANS FOR A PLANT-BASED VERSION.

HONEY GARLIC CHICKEN

INSTRUCTIONS

6 PERSON **4-6 HOURS** **10 MINUTES**

1. Prepare the Chicken: Place the boneless, skinless chicken breasts into the slow cooker.
2. Make the Sauce: In a small bowl, whisk together honey, low-sodium soy sauce, minced garlic, rice vinegar, olive oil, sesame oil (if using), ground black pepper, and red pepper flakes (if using). Pour this mixture over the chicken in the slow cooker.
3. Optional Vegetables: If you'd like to add bell peppers or broccoli, layer them on top of the chicken.
4. Slow Cook: Set your slow cooker to low and cook for 4-6 hours, or until the chicken is tender and cooked through (internal temperature should reach 165°F / 75°C).
   Alternatively, you can cook on high for 2-3 hours if you need the dish to be ready sooner.
   Thicken the Sauce (Optional): If you prefer a thicker sauce, 30 minutes before the cooking time is up, mix 1 tbsp of cornstarch with 1/4 cup of cold water. Stir this slurry into the slow cooker and let it thicken as the cooking finishes.
5. Shred or Serve Whole: Once the chicken is cooked, you can either serve the breasts whole or shred the chicken directly in the slow cooker using two forks. Mix the shredded chicken with the sauce to ensure it's well-coated.

INGREDIENTS

4 boneless, skinless chicken breasts (about 1.5-2 lbs)
1/3 cup honey
1/4 cup low-sodium soy sauce
4 garlic cloves, minced
2 tbsp rice vinegar (or apple cider vinegar)
1 tbsp olive oil
1 tsp sesame oil (optional, for extra flavor)
1/2 tsp ground black pepper
1/4 tsp red pepper flakes (optional, for heat)
1 tbsp cornstarch (optional, for thickening)
1/4 cup cold water (to mix with cornstarch, if thickening)

OPTIONAL ADD-INS

1/2 tsp ginger (fresh or ground)
1 cup sliced bell peppers (for added nutrition)
1 cup broccoli florets (for added fiber)

NUTRITIONAL

Calories: 220 kcal
Protein: 28g
Carbohydrates: 20g
Fat: 5g
Fiber: 1g
Cholesterol: 75mg
Sodium: 490mg
Potassium: 410mg

TOPPINGS AND GARNISHES

Sliced green onions
Sesame seeds
Fresh cilantro
Lime wedges (for a citrusy twist)
Steamed rice or quinoa (as a base)

Health Benefits: Slow cooking locks in nutrients while allowing you to use minimal added fats. The balance of protein from the chicken and the wholesome sweetness of honey offers a nutritious meal that's easy on digestion. Adding vegetables like broccoli boosts fiber content and adds essential vitamins.

Dietary Adjustments: This dish can be easily adapted for those on gluten-free diets by using tamari instead of soy sauce. It's naturally dairy-free, and you can adjust the level of sweetness or spice to your preference.

THIS NOURISHING HONEY GARLIC CHICKEN RECIPE IS PERFECT FOR ANY MEAL OF THE DAY AND CAN BE ENJOYED BY PEOPLE WITH VARIOUS DIETARY PREFERENCES. SLOW COOKING HELPS RETAIN THE NUTRIENTS WHILE CREATING TENDER, FLAVORFUL CHICKEN.

6 PERSON   **8 HOURS**   **15 MINUTES**

INSTRUCTIONS

1. Prepare the Pork:

   Pat the pork shoulder dry with paper towels. Season all sides with salt, pepper, smoked paprika, ground cumin, oregano, and cayenne pepper.

2. Sear the Pork: (Optional but recommended)

   Heat olive oil in a large skillet over medium-high heat. Sear the pork shoulder on all sides until browned (about 2-3 minutes per side). This step adds extra flavor but can be skipped if you're short on time.

3. Prepare the Slow Cooker:

   Place the chopped onion and minced garlic in the bottom of the slow cooker.
   Add any optional additions like chopped bell peppers or apple slices.

4. Mix the Sauce:

   In a bowl, mix the BBQ sauce, chicken broth, apple cider vinegar, brown sugar, Worcestershire sauce, and Dijon mustard. Stir well to combine.

5. Cook the Pork:

   Place the seared (or raw) pork shoulder on top of the onions and garlic in the slow cooker.
   Pour the BBQ sauce mixture over the pork, ensuring it's well coated.

6. Slow Cook:

   Cover and cook on low for 8 hours or on high for 4 hours, until the pork is tender and easily shreds with a fork.

7. Shred the Pork:

   Remove the pork shoulder from the slow cooker and place it on a cutting board. Use two forks to shred the pork into bite-sized pieces.
   Return the shredded pork to the slow cooker and mix well with the sauce. Let it sit on the "keep warm" setting for an additional 30 minutes to absorb flavors.

INGREDIENTS

3 to 4 lbs pork shoulder (or pork butt), trimmed of excess fat
1 large onion, finely chopped
3 cloves garlic, minced
1 cup BBQ sauce (store-bought or homemade)
1 cup low-sodium chicken broth
2 tablespoons apple cider vinegar
2 tablespoons brown sugar
1 tablespoon smoked paprika
1 tablespoon ground cumin
1 teaspoon dried oregano
1/2 teaspoon cayenne pepper (optional, for heat)
1 teaspoon salt
1/2 teaspoon black pepper
1 tablespoon olive oil

OPTIONAL ADDITIONS

1 tablespoon Worcestershire sauce (for added depth)
1 tablespoon Dijon mustard (for tanginess)
1/2 cup chopped bell peppers (for extra veggies)
1/2 cup apple slices (for a hint of sweetness)

TOPPINGS OR GARNISHES

Coleslaw (for crunch)
Pickled onions (for tanginess)
Sliced jalapeños (for extra heat)
Chopped fresh cilantro (for freshness)
Sliced avocado (for creaminess)

NUTRITIONAL

Calories: 350
Protein: 30g
Carbohydrates: 20g
Fat: 15g
Fiber: 2g
Cholesterol: 95mg
Sodium: 750mg
Potassium: 550mg

Enjoy your flavorful and nourishing BBQ pulled pork! It's perfect for sandwiches, tacos, or simply served over a bed of greens.

BBQ PULLED PORK

CONVENIENCE: THE SLOW COOKER MAKES MEAL PREP EASY AND HANDS-OFF, ALLOWING FLAVORS TO DEVELOP FULLY. NUTRITIONAL BALANCE: THIS DISH PROVIDES A GOOD BALANCE OF PROTEIN AND CARBOHYDRATES. ADDING VEGETABLES CAN INCREASE FIBER AND MICRONUTRIENTS.

- CONVENIENCE: SLOW COOKING MAKES THIS DISH A SET-IT-AND-FORGET-IT MEAL, PERFECT FOR BUSY DAYS. SIMPLY PREPARE THE INGREDIENTS, SET THE SLOW COOKER, AND ENJOY A DELICIOUS, NUTRITIOUS MEAL AT THE END OF THE DAY.

- HEALTH BENEFITS: THIS RECIPE FEATURES LEAN BEEF RICH IN PROTEIN, HEARTY VEGETABLES FOR FIBER AND NUTRIENTS, AND THE OPTION TO ADD EXTRA VEGGIES LIKE MUSHROOMS OR ZUCCHINI FOR MORE VITAMINS. THE LOW-SODIUM BROTH HELPS KEEP SODIUM LEVELS IN CHECK, MAKING IT A HEART-HEALTHY OPTION.

EASY BEEF POT ROAST

6 PERSON **8 HOURS** **15 MINUTES**

INSTRUCTIONS

1. Prepare the Beef: - Pat the beef chuck roast dry with paper towels. Season generously with salt, pepper, smoked paprika, and a little olive oil to coat.

2. Sear the Beef (Optional but Recommended): - Heat 2 tablespoons of olive oil in a large skillet over medium-high heat. Sear the beef roast on all sides until browned (about 4-5 minutes per side). This step enhances the flavor but can be skipped if you're short on time.

3. Prepare the Vegetables: - While the beef is searing, chop the onion, carrots, potatoes, celery, and garlic. Place the vegetables in the bottom of the slow cooker, creating a base for the roast.

4. Assemble in the Slow Cooker:
   Place the seared beef chuck roast on top of the vegetables in the slow cooker. In a bowl, whisk together the beef broth, Worcestershire sauce, and tomato paste until smooth. Pour this mixture over the beef and vegetables.
   Add the minced garlic, thyme, rosemary, and bay leaves on top. If you are using any optional additions (like mushrooms, red wine, Dijon mustard, or balsamic vinegar), add them now.

5. Slow Cook:
   For low heat: Set the slow cooker to low and cook for 8 hours.
   For high heat: Set it to high and cook for 4 hours.
   The pot roast is done when the meat is fork-tender and easily shreds. You can test it by pulling a piece with a fork—if it falls apart, it's ready.

INGREDIENTS

3-4 lbs beef chuck roast (trimmed of excess fat)
1 large onion, chopped
4 medium carrots, peeled and cut into chunks
3 medium potatoes, peeled and quartered
3 celery stalks, chopped
4 cloves garlic, minced
2 cups low-sodium beef broth
1 tablespoon Worcestershire sauce
2 tablespoons tomato paste
2 tablespoons olive oil
1 teaspoon dried thyme
1 teaspoon dried rosemary
2 bay leaves
1 teaspoon smoked paprika (optional for extra flavor)
Salt and black pepper, to taste

OPTIONAL ADDITIONS:

1 cup mushrooms, sliced (for extra texture and nutrients)
1 cup red wine (for enhanced depth of flavor)
1 tablespoon Dijon mustard (for a tangy kick)
1 tablespoon balsamic vinegar (for added richness)

NUTRITIONAL

Calories: 400 kcal
Protein: 32g
Carbohydrates: 24g
Fat: 20g
Fiber: 4g
Cholesterol: 110mg
Sodium: 600mg
Potassium: 1000mg

TOPPINGS OR GARNISHES

Fresh parsley or thyme (for added freshness)
Horseradish sauce (for a bit of sharpness)
Crusty bread or mashed potatoes (as a side)

6 PERSON   **4-5 HOURS**   **20 MINUTES**

INSTRUCTIONS

1. Prepare the Meat (or Plant-Based Alternative): In a large skillet over medium heat, cook the ground beef or turkey until browned, breaking it apart with a spoon. If using plant-based crumbles, skip browning and simply warm them.
   Add the chopped onion and garlic to the skillet and cook until soft (about 3-4 minutes). Drain any excess fat and stir in the marinara sauce, diced tomatoes (with their juice), basil, oregano, salt, pepper, and red pepper flakes. Simmer for 5 minutes, then remove from heat.

2. Mix the Ricotta Layer: In a medium bowl, combine the ricotta cheese, Parmesan, egg, and spinach (if using). Mix until well blended.

3. Assemble the Lasagna in the Slow Cooker: Grease the bottom and sides of your slow cooker lightly with cooking spray or olive oil. Spread a thin layer of the meat sauce on the bottom of the slow cooker. Break lasagna noodles to fit in a single layer on top of the sauce. Add a layer of the ricotta mixture, followed by a handful of mozzarella. Repeat the layers: meat sauce, noodles, ricotta mixture, and mozzarella, until all ingredients are used. Aim for about 3-4 layers. End with a final layer of noodles, meat sauce, and mozzarella on top.

4. Add Liquid and Cook: Pour 1/2 cup of water around the edges of the lasagna to ensure moisture during cooking. Cover and cook on low for 4-5 hours, or until the noodles are tender. Avoid lifting the lid during cooking to maintain the heat.

5. Serve and Garnish: Once cooked, turn off the slow cooker and let the lasagna sit for about 15 minutes before slicing to allow it to set. Garnish with fresh parsley and extra Parmesan, if desired.

INGREDIENTS

12 lasagna noodles, uncooked (whole grain or regular)
1 lb ground beef (or turkey for a leaner option; can also use plant-based crumbles for a vegetarian version)
1 medium onion, finely chopped
3 garlic cloves, minced
2 cups marinara sauce (homemade or store-bought, no added sugar preferred)
1 (14.5 oz) can diced tomatoes, with juice
1 tsp dried basil
1 tsp dried oregano
1 tsp salt (adjust to taste)
1/2 tsp black pepper
1/2 tsp red pepper flakes (optional, for a bit of spice)
2 cups ricotta cheese (or cottage cheese for a lighter option)
1 1/2 cups shredded mozzarella cheese
1/2 cup grated Parmesan cheese
1 large egg
2 cups fresh spinach, chopped (optional for added nutrition)
1 cup mushrooms, sliced (optional for added texture)
1/2 cup water (to prevent dryness)
Fresh parsley, chopped (for garnish)

OPTIONAL ADDITIONS

Zucchini or eggplant slices, layered between the lasagna noodles for extra veggies
Sliced bell peppers for more flavor and nutrition

TOPPINGS OR GARNISHES

Fresh basil or parsley
Grated Parmesan cheese
Crushed red pepper flakes for heat
A drizzle of balsamic glaze for sweetness

NUTRITIONAL

Calories: 450
Protein: 28g
Carbohydrates: 40g
Fat: 18g
Saturated Fat: 8g
Fiber: 6g
Cholesterol: 80mg
Sodium: 800mg
Potassium: 600mg

SLOW COOKER
LASAGNA

WHOLE GRAIN LASAGNA NOODLES AND THE ADDITION OF SPIN-
ACH OR ZUCCHINI PROVIDE EXTRA FIBER, PROMOTING DIGES-
TION AND HEART HEALTH.
RICOTTA OR COTTAGE CHEESE OFFERS A GOOD SOURCE OF CAL-
CIUM AND PROTEIN.
USING LEAN GROUND TURKEY OR PLANT-BASED CRUMBLES
MAKES THIS DISH LOWER IN SATURATED FAT, SUITABLE FOR
HEART-HEALTHY DIETS.
SLOW COOKING PRESERVES THE NUTRIENTS IN VEGETABLES
AND MAKES THIS LASAGNA MORE FLAVORFUL, CONVENIENT,
AND PERFECT FOR ANY MEAL!

6 PERSON **4-6 HOURS** **15 MINUTES**

INSTRUCTIONS

1. Prepare the Meat (or Plant-Based Alternative): In a large skillet over medium heat, cook the ground beef or turkey until browned, breaking it apart with a spoon. If using plant-based crumbles, skip browning and simply warm them.
   Add the chopped onion and garlic to the skillet and cook until soft (about 3-4 minutes). Drain any excess fat and stir in the marinara sauce, diced tomatoes (with their juice), basil, oregano, salt, pepper, and red pepper flakes. Simmer for 5 minutes, then remove from heat.

2. Mix the Ricotta Layer: In a medium bowl, combine the ricotta cheese, Parmesan, egg, and spinach (if using). Mix until well blended.

3. Assemble the Lasagna in the Slow Cooker: Grease the bottom and sides of your slow cooker lightly with cooking spray or olive oil. Spread a thin layer of the meat sauce on the bottom of the slow cooker. Break lasagna noodles to fit in a single layer on top of the sauce. Add a layer of the ricotta mixture, followed by a handful of mozzarella. Repeat the layers: meat sauce, noodles, ricotta mixture, and mozzarella, until all ingredients are used. Aim for about 3-4 layers. End with a final layer of noodles, meat sauce, and mozzarella on top.

4. Add Liquid and Cook: Pour 1/2 cup of water around the edges of the lasagna to ensure moisture during cooking. Cover and cook on low for 4-5 hours, or until the noodles are tender. Avoid lifting the lid during cooking to maintain the heat.

5. Serve and Garnish: Once cooked, turn off the slow cooker and let the lasagna sit for about 15 minutes before slicing to allow it to set. Garnish with fresh parsley and extra Parmesan, if desired.

INGREDIENTS

2 medium carrots, peeled and sliced
2 medium potatoes (Yukon Gold or sweet potatoes for a sweeter option), diced
1 medium onion, chopped
1 large bell pepper (any color), chopped
2 cups cauliflower florets
1 cup green beans, trimmed and cut into 1-inch pieces
1 ½ cups canned chickpeas, drained and rinsed
1 ½ cups canned diced tomatoes, with juices
1 can (13.5 oz) coconut milk (full-fat or light depending on preference)
2 cloves garlic, minced
1 tablespoon fresh ginger, grated
2 tablespoons curry powder (mild or medium, depending on heat preference)
1 teaspoon ground cumin
1 teaspoon ground coriander
1 teaspoon turmeric
1 teaspoon salt, or to taste
½ teaspoon black pepper
½ teaspoon red pepper flakes (optional for spice)
1 ½ cups vegetable broth

OPTIONAL ADDITIONS

1 tablespoon garam masala (for extra warmth and depth of flavor)
2 tablespoons peanut butter or almond butter (for added creaminess and protein)
1 cup spinach or kale, chopped (to stir in at the end for extra greens)
1 teaspoon lemon or lime juice (for added brightness before serving)
1 tablespoon maple syrup or honey (for a touch of sweetness, if desired)

TOPPINGS OR GARNISHES

Spoon the vegetable curry into bowls and top with your choice of garnishes such as:

Fresh cilantro
A dollop of plain yogurt (dairy or plant-based)
Chopped peanuts or cashews
Lime wedges
A sprinkle of red chili flakes for extra heat

NUTRITIONAL

Calories: 290
Protein: 8g
Carbohydrates: 40g
Fat: 12g
Fiber: 9g
Cholesterol: 0mg
Sodium: 600mg
Potassium: 950mg

VEGETABLE CURRY

SLOW COOKING PRESERVES THE NUTRIENTS IN VEGETABLES
AND ALLOWS FLAVORS TO DEVELOP FULLY WITH MINIMAL EF-
FORT.
VEGAN AND GLUTEN-FREE: THIS CURRY SUITS A WIDE VARIETY
OF DIETARY PREFERENCES, AND IT'S PACKED WITH PLANT-
BASED PROTEIN AND FIBER FROM CHICKPEAS AND VEGETABLES.
THE ADDITION OF COCONUT MILK GIVES IT A CREAMY TEXTURE
WHILE OFFERING HEALTHY FATS THAT CAN SUPPORT ENERGY
LEVELS THROUGHOUT THE DAY.

CHEESY MASHED POTATOES

INSTRUCTIONS

6 PERSON   **4 HOURS**   **15 MINUTES**

1. Prepare the Potatoes: Peel and cube the potatoes into roughly 1-inch pieces. This helps them cook evenly and become tender more quickly.

2. Add Ingredients to Slow Cooker: Place the cubed potatoes in the slow cooker. Pour in the chicken or vegetable broth, and add the pieces of butter. If using garlic powder and onion powder, add them here. Season with salt and pepper to taste.

3. Cook: Cover the slow cooker with its lid. Set the slow cooker to cook on high for 4 hours or low for 8 hours.

4. Check Potatoes: After the cooking time, check the potatoes by piercing them with a fork. They should be very tender and break apart easily.

5. Mash and Mix: Using a potato masher or an immersion blender, mash the potatoes directly in the slow cooker until smooth. Stir in the milk, sour cream (or Greek yogurt), and shredded cheddar cheese. Continue mixing until everything is well combined and the cheese is melted.

6. Adjust Seasoning: Taste the mashed potatoes and adjust the seasoning with additional salt and pepper if needed.

7. Serve: Transfer the mashed potatoes to a serving dish. Garnish with chopped fresh chives if desired.

INGREDIENTS

2 pounds (900g) potatoes (russet or Yukon gold), peeled and cubed
1 cup (240ml) low-sodium chicken or vegetable broth
1/2 cup (120ml) milk (any variety, including non-dairy alternatives like almond or soy milk)
1/4 cup (60g) unsalted butter, cut into small pieces
1 cup (120g) shredded cheddar cheese (mild or sharp, depending on preference)
1/2 cup (120ml) sour cream (or Greek yogurt for a healthier option)
Salt and pepper, to taste
1/2 teaspoon garlic powder (optional)
1/4 teaspoon onion powder (optional)
1/4 cup (60g) chopped fresh chives (for garnish, optional)

NUTRITIONAL

Calories: 270
Protein: 8g
Carbohydrates: 32g
Fat: 13g
Fiber: 3g
Cholesterol: 35mg
Sodium: 430mg
Potassium: 620mg

TOPPINGS AND GARNISHES

Crumbled bacon for added crunch and flavor
Extra shredded cheese on top
A drizzle of olive oil or a sprinkle of paprika for a bit of color
Sour cream or Greek yogurt for extra creaminess

HEALTH BENEFITS AND CONVENIENCE

Convenience: The slow cooker allows you to prepare the dish in the morning and have it ready by dinner time, making it perfect for busy days.
Nutritional Benefits: Potatoes are a good source of vitamins C and B6, potassium, and dietary fiber. Using low-sodium broth and controlling the amount of added butter and cheese helps keep the dish relatively healthy.
Dietary Adaptations: This recipe is versatile and can be adapted to various dietary preferences by substituting dairy or using a different type of cheese.

ENJOY YOUR
NOURISHING AND
SIMPLE CHEESY
MASHED POTA-
TOES, PERFECT FOR
ANY MEAL OF THE
DAY!

6 PERSON   **2-3 HOURS**   **10 MINUTES**

INSTRUCTIONS

1. Prep the Slow Cooker: Lightly grease the inside of your slow cooker with cooking spray or butter to prevent sticking.
2. Add Ingredients: In the slow cooker, combine the uncooked elbow macaroni, cheddar cheese, mozzarella cheese, butter, whole milk, evaporated milk, garlic powder, onion powder, paprika, Dijon mustard, pepper, and salt. Stir everything together gently.
3. Cover and Cook: Cover the slow cooker and cook on low for 2 to 3 hours, stirring halfway through. Cooking time may vary depending on your slow cooker model, so check after 1.5 hours to ensure it doesn't overcook.
4. Check the Texture: After 2 hours, check the pasta for doneness. The macaroni should be tender, and the sauce should be creamy. If the pasta isn't done, let it cook for another 15-30 minutes.
5. Finish with Optional Ingredients: Once the pasta is cooked, stir in the Greek yogurt or sour cream if using, and fold in any optional additions like steamed broccoli or spinach. Stir well to combine.
6. Serve: Once done, set the slow cooker to warm until ready to serve.

INGREDIENTS

2 medium carrots, peeled and sliced
2 medium potatoes (Yukon Gold or sweet potatoes for a sweeter option), diced
1 medium onion, chopped
1 large bell pepper (any color), chopped
2 cups cauliflower florets
1 cup green beans, trimmed and cut into 1-inch pieces
1 ½ cups canned chickpeas, drained and rinsed
1 ½ cups canned diced tomatoes, with juices
1 can (13.5 oz) coconut milk (full-fat or light depending on preference)
2 cloves garlic, minced
1 tablespoon fresh ginger, grated
2 tablespoons curry powder (mild or medium, depending on heat preference)
1 teaspoon ground cumin
1 teaspoon ground coriander
1 teaspoon turmeric
1 teaspoon salt, or to taste
½ teaspoon black pepper
½ teaspoon red pepper flakes (optional for spice)
1 ½ cups vegetable broth

OPTIONAL ADDITIONS

1 cup steamed broccoli florets or spinach (for added veggies)
1/4 cup grated Parmesan cheese (for extra richness)
1/4 tsp cayenne pepper or hot sauce (for heat)

TOPPINGS OR GARNISHES

Chopped fresh parsley or chives
Crispy bacon bits (optional)
A sprinkle of smoked paprika or black pepper
Extra shredded cheese on top

NUTRITIONAL

Calories: 435 kcal
Protein: 21 g
Carbohydrates: 35 g
Fat: 23 g
Fiber: 2 g
Cholesterol: 88 mg
Sodium: 650 mg
Potassium: 450 mg

HEALTH BENEFITS:

Whole Milk: Adds creaminess and is rich in calcium.
Greek Yogurt: Provides protein and probiotics for digestive health.
Cheese: A good source of protein and calcium.
Broccoli/Spinach (optional): Increases fiber, vitamins, and antioxidants, making it a more balanced meal.

CROCK POT MAC & CHEESE

THIS DISH IS SIMPLE, COMFORTING, AND PACKED WITH NU-
TRIENTS, MAKING IT SUITABLE FOR DIFFERENT DIETARY NEEDS
WITH EASY ADJUSTMENTS.

ENJOY THIS WARM, CREAMY, AND WHOLESOME DISH FOR ANY MEAL, WHETHER AS A SIDE OR A COMFORTING MAIN!

GLUTEN-FREE: THIS DISH IS NATURALLY GLUTEN-FREE, MAKING IT SUITABLE FOR THOSE WITH GLUTEN INTOLERANCE.
VEGETARIAN: BY OMITTING ANIMAL-BASED TOPPINGS AND USING DAIRY-FREE CREAM CHEESE, IT CAN BE MADE VEGAN.
LOW SODIUM: OPT FOR UNSALTED BUTTER AND OMIT ADDED SALT TO LOWER SODIUM CONTENT FOR THOSE ON A LOW-SODIUM DIET.
HIGH FIBER: ADDING BELL PEPPERS OR NUTRITIONAL YEAST BOOSTS FIBER CONTENT, MAKING IT A MORE FILLING AND NUTRIENT-DENSE DISH.

CREAMED CORN

6 PERSON   **3-4 HOURS**   **10 MINUTES**

INSTRUCTIONS

1. Prepare the Slow Cooker:
    Lightly grease the inside of the slow cooker with cooking spray or a small amount of butter to prevent sticking.
2. Add the Ingredients:
    Pour the corn into the slow cooker. Add the half-and-half, cream cheese, butter, garlic powder, onion powder, and sugar (if using). Stir gently to distribute the ingredients evenly.
3. Cook on Low or High:
    For a slower cook, set the slow cooker to low and cook for 6-7 hours.
    For a faster cook, set it to high and cook for 3-4 hours. Stir halfway through cooking to ensure even melting of the cream cheese and butter.
4. Final Steps:
    About 15 minutes before serving, stir the creamed corn thoroughly. If you prefer a thicker consistency, use a potato masher or immersion blender to mash part of the corn, leaving some whole kernels for texture.
5. Season and Serve:
    Taste and adjust the seasoning with salt and pepper. If you're using optional ingredients like fresh herbs, Parmesan, or nutritional yeast, stir them in now.

INGREDIENTS

5 cups frozen or fresh corn kernels (about 1.5 pounds)
1 cup half-and-half (or substitute with unsweetened almond milk for a lighter version)
4 oz cream cheese (reduced-fat or dairy-free, if preferred), cubed
¼ cup unsalted butter, cubed
2 tbsp sugar or honey (optional for natural sweetness)
1 tsp garlic powder
½ tsp onion powder
Salt and pepper to taste

OPTIONAL ADDITIONS:

1 tbsp fresh chopped thyme or parsley
¼ cup grated Parmesan cheese (optional, for richer flavor)
1 diced jalapeño for a bit of spice
1 cup diced bell peppers for added crunch and vitamins
¼ cup nutritional yeast for a vegan-friendly, cheesy flavor

NUTRITIONAL

Calories: 220 kcal
Protein: 4.5 g
Carbohydrates: 27 g
Fat: 12 g
Fiber: 3 g
Cholesterol: 35 mg
Sodium: 220 mg
Potassium: 300 mg

TOPPINGS OR GARNISHES

Freshly chopped parsley or chives
A sprinkle of smoked paprika or chili flakes for heat
Grated cheese (Parmesan, cheddar, or dairy-free alternative)
Crumbled bacon or plant-based bacon bits for crunch

4 PERSON   **2-3 HOURS**   **10 MINUTES**

INSTRUCTIONS

1. Prepare the green beans:
    Trim and wash the fresh green beans. If you prefer, you can cut them into smaller bite-sized pieces.
2. Assemble in the slow cooker:
    In your slow cooker, add the green beans, minced garlic, vegetable or chicken broth, olive oil, sea salt, black pepper, and red pepper flakes (if using).
3. Slow cook the green beans:
    Stir to coat the green beans with the seasoning and broth. Set your slow cooker to the low setting and cook for 2.5 to 3 hours, or until the green beans are tender but still slightly crisp. For softer beans, you can cook up to 4 hours.
4. Finishing touches:
    About 10 minutes before the cooking time ends, sprinkle 2 tbsp of Parmesan cheese over the green beans. Stir gently to combine, allowing the cheese to melt into the dish.
5. Optional flavor boost:
    Just before serving, squeeze 1 tbsp of fresh lemon juice over the green beans for a bright, fresh flavor. This is optional but highly recommended for added depth.
6. Serving:
    Transfer the green beans to a serving dish. Garnish with additional grated Parmesan, slivered almonds or chopped walnuts if using, and a sprinkle of red pepper flakes or smoked paprika for extra flavor.

INGREDIENTS

1 lb (450g) fresh green beans, trimmed
4 cloves garlic, minced
1/4 cup (60 ml) low-sodium vegetable or chicken broth
1 tbsp (15 ml) olive oil
2 tbsp (30g) grated Parmesan cheese (plus more for garnish if desired)
1/2 tsp (2.5g) sea salt (adjust to taste)
1/4 tsp (1g) black pepper
1/4 tsp (1g) red pepper flakes (optional, for a slight kick)
1 tbsp fresh lemon juice (optional, for a bright flavor boost)

OPTIONAL ADDITIONS

1/4 cup (30g) slivered almonds or chopped walnuts (for added crunch and healthy fats)
1/4 tsp smoked paprika (for a deeper, smoky flavor)

TOPPINGS OR GARNISHES

Extra Parmesan cheese
Fresh parsley or thyme
Crushed red pepper flakes for heat
Toasted almonds or walnuts for texture

NUTRITIONAL

Calories: 130
Protein: 5g
Carbohydrates: 10g
Fat: 8g
Fiber: 4g
Cholesterol: 4mg
Sodium: 350mg
Potassium: 290mg

HEALTH BENEFITS

This slow cooker recipe is low in calories and rich in fiber, making it ideal for weight management and digestive health. The olive oil and optional nuts provide healthy fats, while green beans are packed with vitamins like A, C, and K. Slow cooking allows the garlic to fully infuse the dish with flavor while keeping the beans tender and nutritious.

GARLIC PARMESAN
GREEN BEANS

THIS SIMPLE AND NOURISHING RECIPE FOR GARLIC PARMESAN GREEN BEANS IS PERFECT FOR ANY MEAL. IT OFFERS CONVENIENCE AND FLAVOR WITH MINIMAL EFFORT. THIS HEALTHY SIDE DISH IS PACKED WITH NUTRIENTS AND CAN BE CUSTOMIZED TO SUIT VARIOUS DIETARY PREFERENCES.

8 PERSON **4 HOURS** **15 MINUTES**

INSTRUCTIONS

1. Prepare the bread cubes: If your bread isn't already cubed, cut it into 1-inch cubes. If it's too soft, you can toast it in the oven at 300°F (150°C) for about 15 minutes until slightly crisp.

2. Mix the ingredients: In a large bowl, combine the bread cubes, onion, celery, carrots (if using), garlic, parsley, sage, thyme, salt, and pepper. If you want additional flavor or texture, stir in the walnuts and cranberries at this stage.

3. Add the liquid: Drizzle the melted butter (or oil) over the mixture and toss to coat evenly. Then, pour the broth over the bread mixture, stirring gently to combine. The bread should be moist but not soggy—add a little more broth if needed.

4. Prepare the slow cooker: Lightly grease the inside of your slow cooker with cooking spray or oil. Transfer the stuffing mixture into the slow cooker, pressing it down gently with a spoon.

5. Cook the stuffing: Cover and cook on low for 4 hours. If your slow cooker runs hot, check after 3.5 hours to ensure the stuffing isn't burning. The stuffing should be moist and fluffy, with a golden crust around the edges.

6. Finishing touches: Once done, fluff the stuffing with a fork and adjust the seasoning if necessary. For a crispier top, you can remove the lid for the last 30 minutes of cooking.

INGREDIENTS

12 cups bread cubes (whole wheat or gluten-free)
1 cup onion, finely chopped
1 cup celery, finely chopped
1/2 cup carrots, diced (optional for extra nutrition)
2 cloves garlic, minced
1/2 cup unsalted butter, melted (or coconut oil for dairy-free)
2 1/2 cups low-sodium vegetable broth (or chicken broth for non-vegetarian)
1/4 cup fresh parsley, chopped
1 tbsp fresh sage, chopped (or 1 tsp dried sage)
1 tbsp fresh thyme, chopped (or 1 tsp dried thyme)
1/2 tsp black pepper
1/4 tsp salt (optional, depending on broth sodium content)
1/2 cup chopped walnuts or pecans (optional for extra crunch)
1/2 cup dried cranberries (optional for sweetness)

TOPPINGS OR GARNISHES

Fresh parsley or thyme sprigs
A drizzle of olive oil or balsamic glaze
Grated Parmesan (if not dairy-free)

NUTRITIONAL

Calories: 250
Protein: 5g
Carbohydrates: 35g
Fat: 10g
Fiber: 5g
Cholesterol: 15mg
Sodium: 320mg
Potassium: 220mg

SLOW COOKER
STUFFING

THIS SLOW COOKER STUFFING IS A SIMPLE, NUTRITIOUS MEAL THAT HIGHLIGHTS THE BENEFITS OF SLOW COOKING, INCLUDING ENHANCED FLAVOR AND CONVENIENCE. IT'S CUSTOMIZABLE FOR VARIOUS DIETARY NEEDS (E.G., VEGAN, GLUTEN-FREE) AND PROVIDES A HEARTY BALANCE OF FIBER, HEALTHY FATS, AND CARBOHYDRATES.

LENTIL SOUP

INSTRUCTIONS

6 PERSON **8 HOURS** **15 MINUTES**

1. Prepare Ingredients: Rinse the lentils under cold water and set aside.
   Dice the onion, garlic, carrots, celery, and red bell pepper.

2. Sauté Aromatics (Optional but recommended): Heat the olive oil in a skillet over medium heat.
   Add the diced onion and garlic, sautéing until translucent and fragrant (about 3-5 minutes).
   Transfer the sautéed onion and garlic to the slow cooker. This step enhances the flavor, but you can skip it for a simpler preparation.

3. Combine Ingredients in Slow Cooker: Add the rinsed lentils, diced carrots, celery, red bell pepper, and diced tomatoes to the slow cooker.
   Pour in the vegetable broth.
   Stir in the bay leaf, ground cumin, paprika, dried thyme, turmeric (if using), black pepper, and salt.

4. Cook: Set the slow cooker to low for 8 hours or high for 4 hours.
   If using fresh spinach or kale, add it during the last 30 minutes of cooking for added nutrition and freshness.

5. Final Adjustments: Remove the bay leaf before serving.
   Adjust seasoning with more salt, pepper, or a splash of lemon juice if desired.

INGREDIENTS

1 cup dried brown or green lentils, rinsed and drained
1 large onion, diced
2 cloves garlic, minced
3 carrots, peeled and diced
2 celery stalks, diced
1 red bell pepper, diced
1 can (14.5 oz) diced tomatoes, with juices
4 cups vegetable broth (or chicken broth for non-vegetarian)
1 bay leaf
1 teaspoon ground cumin
1 teaspoon paprika
1 teaspoon dried thyme
1/2 teaspoon turmeric (optional, for extra flavor and color)
1/2 teaspoon black pepper
1/2 teaspoon salt (adjust to taste)
1 cup fresh spinach or kale, chopped (optional, added in the last 30 minutes)
1 tablespoon olive oil (optional, for sautéing)

OPTIONAL ADDITIONS

1 tablespoon soy sauce or tamari (for a umami flavor boost)
1/2 cup diced potatoes (for extra heartiness)
1 teaspoon lemon juice (added just before serving for a bright flavor)

NUTRITIONAL

Calories: 220
Protein: 12g
Carbohydrates: 35g
Fat: 3g
Fiber: 12g
Cholesterol: 0mg
Sodium: 600mg
Potassium: 680mg

TOPPINGS AND GARNISHES

Chopped fresh parsley or cilantro
A dollop of Greek yogurt or a sprinkle of shredded cheese
Croutons or a slice of whole-grain bread on the side
A drizzle of extra virgin olive oil for added richness

THIS SLOW COOK-
ER LENTIL SOUP
IS NOT ONLY EASY
TO PREPARE BUT
ALSO A COMFORT-
ING, NUTRITIOUS
CHOICE FOR ANY
MEAL. ENJOY!

CONVENIENCE: THE SLOW COOKER DOES ALL THE WORK, ALLOWING
YOU TO SET IT AND FORGET IT, FREEING UP TIME FOR OTHER TASKS.
NUTRITIONAL VALUE: LENTILS ARE AN EXCELLENT SOURCE OF PRO-
TEIN, FIBER, AND ESSENTIAL NUTRIENTS, MAKING THIS SOUP BOTH
FILLING AND NUTRITIOUS.
CUSTOMIZABLE: THE RECIPE CAN BE ADAPTED TO SUIT VARIOUS DI-
ETARY NEEDS AND PREFERENCES BY MODIFYING OR ADDING INGRE-
DIENTS.

6 PERSON

6-8 HOURS

15 MINUTES

INSTRUCTIONS

1. Prepare Ingredients: Peel and cube the sweet potatoes. Dice the onion, and mince the garlic and ginger.

2. Sauté Aromatics (Optional): In a pan over medium heat, add olive oil. Sauté the onion until it becomes translucent, about 5 minutes.
Add garlic and ginger, cooking for an additional 1-2 minutes until fragrant. This step adds depth to the flavor but can be skipped for a quicker preparation.

3. Combine Ingredients in Slow Cooker: Place the cubed sweet potatoes, chickpeas, diced tomatoes, coconut milk, and sautéed aromatics (if using) into the slow cooker.

4. Add Spices: Sprinkle the curry powder, cumin, paprika, turmeric, coriander, and cayenne pepper (if using) over the ingredients in the slow cooker. Add salt and black pepper.

5. Mix and Cook: Stir everything together to ensure the spices are well distributed.
Cover the slow cooker and set it to cook:
Low: for 6-8 hours
High: for 3-4 hours

6. Add Optional Ingredients: If using spinach, peas, or lime juice, add these during the last 30 minutes of cooking.

7. Check and Adjust: Before serving, check the seasoning and adjust salt and pepper as needed. Stir gently to combine.

8. Serve: Garnish with chopped cilantro and a squeeze of lime juice if desired.

INGREDIENTS

3 medium sweet potatoes, peeled and cubed (about 4 cups)
1 can (15 oz) chickpeas, drained and rinsed
1 large onion, diced
2 cloves garlic, minced
1 tablespoon ginger, minced
1 can (14.5 oz) diced tomatoes, with their juice
1 cup coconut milk (full-fat or light, as preferred)
1 tablespoon curry powder
1 teaspoon ground cumin
1 teaspoon paprika
1/2 teaspoon turmeric
1/2 teaspoon ground coriander
1/4 teaspoon cayenne pepper (optional, for heat)
1 teaspoon salt (or to taste)
1/2 teaspoon black pepper
1 tablespoon olive oil (optional, for sautéing)
1 cup fresh spinach (optional, added in the last 30 minutes of cooking)

OPTIONAL ADDITIONS

1/2 cup frozen peas (added in the last 30 minutes of cooking)
1 tablespoon lime juice (for added brightness, added at the end)
1/4 cup chopped cilantro (for garnish)

TOPPINGS OR GARNISHES

Chopped cilantro
A squeeze of lime juice
Freshly cooked rice or quinoa
Plain yogurt or coconut yogurt for a creamy addition
Toasted cashews or almonds for crunch

NUTRITIONAL

Calories: 290
Protein: 7g
Carbohydrates: 45g
Fat: 10g
Fiber: 9g
Cholesterol: 0mg
Sodium: 450mg
Potassium: 850mg

Nourishing: This recipe is rich in vitamins and minerals from sweet potatoes and chickpeas, offering a good balance of carbohydrates, protein, and healthy fats.
Convenient: The slow cooker does the hard work, allowing you to set it and forget it. Ideal for busy days or meal prepping.
Versatile: This curry is vegan and gluten-free, making it suitable for a variety of dietary preferences.

SWEET POTATO & CHICKPEA CURRY

ENJOY YOUR WHOLESOME, FLAVORFUL SWEET POTATO & CHICK-PEA CURRY AS A COMFORTING MEAL ANYTIME OF THE DAY!

6 PERSON   **6 HOURS**   **20 MINUTES**

INSTRUCTIONS

1. Prep Ingredients: Dice the bell pepper and onion, and mince the garlic.
   If using fresh tomatoes, chop them into small pieces.
2. Layer the Ingredients: In the slow cooker, combine the black beans, diced tomatoes, corn, bell pepper, onion, garlic, and chopped spinach or kale (if using).
   Stir in the ground cumin, chili powder, paprika, smoked paprika (if using), and salt and pepper.
3. Assemble Enchiladas: Pour a small amount of enchilada sauce (about 1/4 cup) at the bottom of the slow cooker and spread it evenly.
   Take a tortilla, sprinkle some shredded cheese in the middle, and add a portion of the black bean mixture.
   Roll up the tortilla and place it seam-side down in the slow cooker. Repeat with the remaining tortillas and mixture.
   Pour the remaining enchilada sauce evenly over the rolled tortillas.
4. Cook: Cover and cook on low for 6 hours or on high for 3 hours. The enchiladas are done when the tortillas are soft and the cheese is melted.
5. Final Touches: If desired, sprinkle additional shredded cheese on top 15 minutes before the cooking time is up, and allow it to melt.

INGREDIENTS

2 cans (15 oz each) black beans, drained and rinsed
1 can (15 oz) diced tomatoes (or 2 cups fresh tomatoes, chopped)
1 cup corn kernels (fresh, frozen, or canned)
1 bell pepper, diced (red, yellow, or green)
1 small onion, finely chopped
2 cloves garlic, minced
1 cup shredded cheese (cheddar or Monterey Jack)
8 small corn or flour tortillas
1 cup enchilada sauce (store-bought or home-made)
1 tsp ground cumin
1 tsp chili powder
1/2 tsp paprika
1/2 tsp smoked paprika (optional)
Salt and pepper to taste

OPTIONAL ADDITIONS

1 cup chopped spinach or kale for extra nutrients
1/2 cup sliced black olives
1/2 cup chopped cilantro

TOPPINGS OR GARNISHES

Fresh cilantro, chopped
Sliced avocado or guacamole
Sour cream or Greek yogurt
Fresh lime wedges
Sliced jalapeños for extra heat
Salsa or pico de gallo

NUTRITIONAL

Calories: 280
Protein: 14g
Carbohydrates: 40g
Fat: 8g
Fiber: 10g
Cholesterol: 20mg
Sodium: 750mg
Potassium: 800mg

Convenience: The slow cooker allows you to prepare this meal in advance, and it does the cooking for you while you go about your day.
Flavor: Slow cooking helps meld flavors together, making the dish more flavorful.
Nutritional Value: Using black beans provides a good source of protein and fiber, while vegetables add vitamins and minerals. Optional greens can boost the nutritional content further.

BLACK BEAN
ENCHILADAS

THIS RECIPE IS VERSATILE AND CAN BE TAILORED TO SUIT VAR-
IOUS DIETARY NEEDS, WHETHER YOU PREFER VEGAN OPTIONS,
GLUTEN-FREE TORTILLAS, OR ADDITIONAL TOPPINGS. ENJOY
THIS NOURISHING MEAL AT ANY TIME OF DAY!

ENJOY THIS EASY
AND NUTRITIOUS
VEGAN QUINOA
CHILI, PERFECT
FOR ANY MEAL OF
THE DAY!

QUINOA IS A COMPLETE PROTEIN AND PROVIDES ALL NINE ESSENTIAL AMINO
ACIDS.
BEANS OFFER A HIGH FIBER CONTENT, AIDING DIGESTION AND PROMOTING
SATIETY.
VEGETABLES CONTRIBUTE VITAMINS, MINERALS, AND ANTIOXIDANTS.
SLOW COOKING ALLOWS FLAVORS TO MELD TOGETHER, MAKING IT A CON-
VENIENT WAY TO PREPARE A NUTRITIOUS AND HEARTY MEAL WITH MINIMAL
EFFORT.

VEGAN QUINOA CHILI

6 PERSON   **6-8 HOURS**   **15 MINUTES**

INSTRUCTIONS

1. Prepare Ingredients: Rinse quinoa under cold water and set aside.
   Dice onion, garlic, bell pepper, carrots, celery, and zucchini.
2. Sauté Vegetables (Optional): In a skillet, heat olive oil over medium heat.
   Add diced onion and garlic; sauté for 3-4 minutes until translucent.
   Add bell pepper, carrots, and celery; cook for an additional 5 minutes.
   This step adds depth of flavor but can be skipped for a quicker prep.
3. Combine Ingredients in Slow Cooker: Place the rinsed quinoa in the slow cooker.
   Add the sautéed vegetables (if using), or directly add raw vegetables if skipping
   the sauté step.
   Stir in diced tomatoes, black beans, kidney beans, corn, and vegetable broth.
   Add tomato paste, chili powder, cumin, paprika, oregano, cayenne pepper (if
   using), salt, and black pepper.
   Mix everything together well to ensure the quinoa is evenly distributed and the
   spices are well incorporated.
4. Cook: Cover the slow cooker with the lid.
   Set to low for 6-8 hours or high for 3-4 hours.
   About 30 minutes before serving, stir in frozen spinach or kale if using.
5. Finish and Serve: Taste and adjust seasoning if necessary.
   Ladle chili into bowls and garnish with avocado slices, chopped cilantro, and
   shredded vegan cheese if desired.

INGREDIENTS

1 cup quinoa, rinsed
1 tablespoon olive oil
1 medium onion, diced
3 cloves garlic, minced
1 large bell pepper, diced (any color)
2 medium carrots, diced
2 stalks celery, diced
1 zucchini, diced
1 (14.5 oz) can diced tomatoes
1 (15 oz) can black beans, drained and rinsed
1 (15 oz) can kidney beans, drained and rinsed
1 (15 oz) can corn kernels, drained
1 cup vegetable broth (low sodium preferred)
2 tablespoons tomato paste
2 tablespoons chili powder
1 tablespoon ground cumin
1 teaspoon paprika
1/2 teaspoon dried oregano
1/4 teaspoon cayenne pepper (optional for heat)
Salt and black pepper, to taste
1 cup frozen spinach or kale, thawed and chopped (optional for added greens)

OPTIONAL ADDITIONS:

1 tablespoon nutritional yeast (for a cheesy flavor)
1 teaspoon smoked paprika (for a smoky flavor)
1 avocado, sliced (for garnish)
1/4 cup chopped fresh cilantro (for garnish)
1/2 cup shredded vegan cheese (for garnish)

NUTRITIONAL

Calories: 290
Protein: 11g
Carbohydrates: 46g
Fat: 8g
Fiber: 8g
Cholesterol: 0mg
Sodium: 580mg
Potassium: 800mg

TOPPINGS OR GARNISHES

Avocado slices: Adds creaminess and healthy fats.
Chopped fresh cilantro: Enhances freshness.
Shredded vegan cheese: Adds a cheesy flavor.
Crushed tortilla chips: For added crunch.

6 PERSON **6-8 HOURS** **20 MINUTES**

INSTRUCTIONS

1. Prepare the Bell Peppers: Wash and cut the tops off the bell peppers. Remove the seeds and membranes from inside. Set aside.
2. Cook the Filling: Heat olive oil in a large skillet over medium heat.
    Add chopped onions and cook for about 3-4 minutes until translucent.
    Add minced garlic and cook for an additional 1 minute.
    Add ground turkey (or beef/chicken) and cook until browned, breaking it up with a spoon as it cooks.
    Stir in cooked quinoa, black beans, corn, diced tomatoes, cumin, smoked paprika, chili powder, oregano, salt, and pepper.
    Cook for another 5 minutes until everything is well combined and heated through. Remove from heat.
3. Stuff the Peppers: Carefully spoon the filling mixture into each bell pepper, packing it in tightly.
    Place the stuffed peppers upright in the slow cooker.
4. Cook in the Slow Cooker: Cover and cook on low for 6-8 hours or on high for 4 hours.
    In the last 30 minutes of cooking, sprinkle the shredded cheese on top of each stuffed pepper.
5. Optional Garnish: If desired, top with fresh cilantro and a dollop of salsa before serving.

INGREDIENTS

6 large bell peppers (any color)
1 pound (450g) ground turkey (or ground beef/chicken for variation)
1 cup cooked quinoa (or brown rice)
1 cup black beans, drained and rinsed
1 cup corn kernels (fresh, frozen, or canned)
1 cup diced tomatoes (canned or fresh)
1/2 cup finely chopped onion
2 cloves garlic, minced
1 cup shredded cheddar cheese (or your favorite cheese)
1 tablespoon olive oil
1 teaspoon ground cumin
1 teaspoon smoked paprika
1/2 teaspoon chili powder
1/2 teaspoon dried oregano
Salt and pepper, to taste

OPTIONAL ADDITIONS

1/2 cup chopped fresh cilantro (for garnish)
1/2 cup salsa (for extra flavor)

NUTRITIONAL

Calories: 290
Protein: 23g
Carbohydrates: 30g
Fat: 8g
Fiber: 8g
Cholesterol: 75mg
Sodium: 450mg
Potassium: 900mg

Slow Cooking Benefits: Slow cooking retains more nutrients and allows flavors to meld beautifully. It also requires minimal hands-on time, making it a convenient option for busy days.
Customizable: Feel free to adjust the ingredients based on dietary preferences or what you have on hand. You can use ground meat alternatives, different grains, or additional vegetables.
Freezing: These stuffed peppers freeze well. To freeze, cook and cool them completely, then wrap each pepper individually in plastic wrap and store in an airtight container. Reheat in the microwave or oven when ready to eat.

STUFFED BELL
PEPPERS

**ENJOY THIS NOURISHING AND VERSATILE DISH
THAT'S PERFECT FOR ANY MEAL OF THE DAY!**

CHICKEN AND RICE CASSEROLE

INSTRUCTIONS

6 PERSON　　　**4-6 HOURS**　　　**15 MINUTES**

1. Prep Ingredients: Rinse the brown rice under cold water and set aside.
   Dice the chicken into large chunks and chop the vegetables (onion, garlic, carrots, and celery). If you're using fresh broccoli, chop it into small florets.

2. Layer the Slow Cooker: Lightly grease the inside of your slow cooker with cooking spray or olive oil.
   Add the diced chicken, uncooked brown rice, onion, garlic, carrots, celery, and any additional vegetables (like mushrooms or peas) into the slow cooker.

3. Add the Liquids and Spices: Pour in the chicken broth and water over the ingredients. Stir in the thyme, oregano, smoked paprika, black pepper, salt, and garlic powder.
   Mix everything gently to distribute the flavors evenly.

4. Set the Slow Cooker: Cover the slow cooker and set it to high for 4–5 hours or low for 7–8 hours. The chicken should be cooked through and the rice should be tender when done.

5. Add Optional Vegetables and Cheese: About 30 minutes before serving, stir in the broccoli florets (if using) and allow them to steam in the slow cooker. For a cheesy casserole, sprinkle shredded cheddar cheese over the top in the last 15 minutes, allowing it to melt before serving.

6. Serve and Garnish: When the casserole is ready, give it a gentle stir and taste for seasoning. Add more salt or pepper if needed. For added brightness, drizzle with lemon juice and garnish with fresh chopped parsley or cilantro.

INGREDIENTS

Main Ingredients:
- 1 ½ lbs (680g) boneless, skinless chicken breasts or thighs, cut into large chunks
- 1 cup long-grain brown rice (uncooked)
- 1 ½ cups low-sodium chicken broth (or vegetable broth for variation)
- 1 cup water
- 1 medium onion, finely diced
- 2 cloves garlic, minced
- 1 cup diced carrots (about 2 medium carrots)
- 1 cup diced celery (about 2 stalks)
- 1 cup fresh or frozen peas (optional for added veggies)
- 1 cup broccoli florets (optional, added in the last 30 minutes)
- 1 cup shredded cheddar cheese (optional, for topping)

SPICES & SEASONING

- 1 tsp dried thyme
- 1 tsp dried oregano
- 1 tsp smoked paprika
- 1 tsp ground black pepper
- ½ tsp salt (adjust to taste)
- 1 tsp garlic powder (optional for extra flavor)

OPTIONAL ADDITIONS

- ½ cup sliced mushrooms (for extra texture)
- 1 tbsp lemon juice (added before serving for brightness)
- ¼ cup chopped fresh parsley or cilantro (for garnish)

NUTRITIONAL

Calories: 300
Protein: 25g
Carbohydrates: 40g
Fat: 6g
Fiber: 5g
Cholesterol: 65mg
Sodium: 420mg
Potassium: 580mg

TOPPINGS AND GARNISHES

Fresh parsley or cilantro, chopped
A drizzle of lemon juice for a fresh, tangy flavor
Extra shredded cheese (cheddar, mozzarella, or Parmesan)
Crushed tortilla chips for a crunchy topping
A dollop of sour cream or Greek yogurt for creaminess

THIS DISH IS A COMFORTING, WELL-ROUNDED MEAL PERFECT FOR ANY TIME OF DAY!

THIS SLOW COOKER CHICKEN AND RICE CASSEROLE IS NOT ONLY CONVENIENT BUT ALSO PACKED WITH NUTRIENTS. USING WHOLE GRAINS LIKE BROWN RICE PROVIDES COMPLEX CARBOHYDRATES AND FIBER, WHILE THE CHICKEN OFFERS LEAN PROTEIN. THE ADDITION OF VEGETABLES BOOSTS THE VITAMIN AND MINERAL CONTENT, AND THE SLOW-COOKING PROCESS ENHANCES FLAVOR WITHOUT NEEDING EXCESS FATS OR SODIUM. FOR THOSE FOLLOWING VEGETARIAN OR GLUTEN-FREE DIETS, EASY SUBSTITUTIONS LIKE VEGETABLE BROTH AND DAIRY-FREE CHEESE ARE GREAT OPTIONS.

6 PERSON **4-6 HOURS** **15 MINUTES**

INSTRUCTIONS

1. Preheat the sausages (optional but recommended for deeper flavor): Heat a skillet over medium heat and add 1 tablespoon of olive oil. Brown the sausage links for 2-3 minutes on each side until they have a golden color but are not fully cooked through. This adds flavor but can be skipped to save time.

2. Layer vegetables in the slow cooker: Place the sliced bell peppers and onions at the bottom of the slow cooker. Add the minced garlic and any optional vegetables (zucchini, mushrooms, etc.).

3. Add seasonings and liquids: Sprinkle the oregano, basil, smoked paprika, and red pepper flakes over the vegetables. Season with salt and pepper to taste. Pour the diced tomatoes (including their juice) and the chicken or vegetable broth over the vegetables. Add the balsamic vinegar if using.

4. Place sausages on top: Lay the browned sausages on top of the vegetable mixture. This allows them to absorb all the flavors as they cook.

5. Cook: Cover the slow cooker and cook on Low for 6 hours or on High for 4 hours. Check occasionally to ensure the sausages are fully cooked (internal temperature should reach 160°F / 70°C for pork or chicken sausage).

6. Optional final steps: During the last 15 minutes of cooking, you can stir in baby spinach for added greens. The spinach will wilt into the dish.

7. Serve: Serve the sausage and peppers on their own, or pair them with whole grain bread, pasta, quinoa, or cauliflower rice for a balanced meal.

INGREDIENTS

1 lb (450g) Italian sausage links (pork, chicken, or turkey for leaner options)
3 bell peppers (red, yellow, green), sliced
1 large yellow onion, sliced
3 cloves garlic, minced
1 can (14.5 oz / 400g) diced tomatoes, undrained
1 tablespoon olive oil
1 teaspoon dried oregano
1 teaspoon dried basil
1 teaspoon smoked paprika
1/2 teaspoon red pepper flakes (optional, for heat)
Salt and pepper to taste
1/4 cup low-sodium chicken or vegetable broth
1 tablespoon balsamic vinegar (optional, for added depth of flavor)

OPTIONAL ADDITIONS

1 zucchini, sliced (adds more vegetables and fiber)
1 cup baby spinach (stir in during the last 15 minutes)
1/2 cup sliced mushrooms
1/4 teaspoon fennel seeds (adds a classic Italian sausage flavor)

TOPPINGS & GARNISHES

Fresh parsley or basil, chopped
Grated Parmesan cheese
Red pepper flakes for extra heat
Squeeze of fresh lemon juice for brightness

NUTRITIONAL

Calories: 320 kcal
Protein: 17g
Carbohydrates: 15g
Fat: 22g
Fiber: 4g
Cholesterol: 50mg
Sodium: 800mg
Potassium: 600mg

This dish is adaptable to a variety of dietary preferences. Use chicken or turkey sausage for a leaner version, add extra vegetables for more fiber and vitamins, or serve with low-carb alternatives for those on keto or gluten-free diets. Slow cooking enhances the flavors and retains nutrients in the vegetables, making this a wholesome meal.

SAUSAGE AND
PEPPERS

ENJOY THIS SIMPLE, NOURISHING, AND FLAVORFUL DISH ANY
TIME OF DAY!

6 PERSON   **4-6 HOURS**   **15 MINUTES**

INSTRUCTIONS

1. Prep the Ingredients: Begin by chopping all vegetables (onion, bell peppers, celery) and slicing the sausage. Cube the chicken and, if using, clean the shrimp.

2. Layer the Ingredients in the Slow Cooker: Start by placing the cubed chicken and sausage in the bottom of the slow cooker. Add the chopped onions, peppers, celery, garlic, and diced tomatoes (with their juice) on top. Sprinkle in the Cajun seasoning, thyme, paprika, smoked paprika, cayenne, salt, and black pepper over the vegetables and protein.

3. Add the Liquids: Pour in the chicken broth and add the tomato paste, stirring lightly to combine. Ensure the rice is evenly submerged in the broth.

4. Cooking Instructions: Low setting: Cook on Low for 4–6 hours.
   High setting: Cook on High for 2–3 hours.
   About 30 minutes before the end of cooking, stir in the shrimp and any other optional ingredients like okra or peas (if using).

5. Final Adjustments:Once the rice is tender and the chicken is fully cooked, turn off the slow cooker. Taste and adjust seasoning with additional salt, pepper, or Cajun seasoning if needed.

6. Serve: Ladle the jambalaya into bowls and garnish with fresh parsley or green onions for extra flavor and color.

INGREDIENTS

Protein:
1 lb (450 g) boneless, skinless chicken breasts, cubed (or chicken thighs for richer flavor)
8 oz (225 g) smoked sausage (Andouille or turkey sausage), sliced
1/2 lb (225 g) shrimp, peeled and deveined (optional, add in the last 30 minutes)
Vegetables:
1 medium onion, chopped
1 medium green bell pepper, chopped
1 medium red bell pepper, chopped
3 celery stalks, chopped
4 cloves garlic, minced
1 (14.5 oz) can diced tomatoes with juice
1 cup diced tomatoes (optional, for more texture)
Carbohydrates:
1 cup uncooked long-grain brown rice (or white rice if preferred)
Spices:
2 tsp Cajun or Creole seasoning (adjust to taste)
1 tsp dried thyme
1 tsp paprika
1/2 tsp smoked paprika (optional)
1/4 tsp cayenne pepper (optional for heat)
Salt and black pepper to taste
Liquids:
2 cups low-sodium chicken broth
1 tbsp tomato paste

OPTIONAL ADDITIONS

1 zucchini, sliced (adds more vegetables and fiber)
1 cup baby spinach (stir in during the last 15 minutes)
1/2 cup sliced mushrooms
1/4 teaspoon fennel seeds (adds a classic Italian sausage flavor)

TOPPINGS & GARNISHES

Fresh parsley or green onions
A splash of hot sauce
Lemon wedges for added brightness

NUTRITIONAL

Calories: 380 kcal
Protein: 32 g
Carbohydrates: 38 g
Fat: 10 g
Saturated Fat: 3 g
Fiber: 5 g
Cholesterol: 120 mg
Sodium: 800 mg
Potassium: 650 mg

For a vegetarian/vegan version: Omit the chicken, sausage, and shrimp. Use beans (such as kidney or black beans) for a plant-based protein and vegetable broth instead of chicken broth.
Health Benefits: Slow cooking preserves the nutrients of vegetables while using less oil, making this recipe nutrient-dense and heart-healthy. Adjust the sodium by using low-sodium broth and controlling seasoning levels.
Convenience: This recipe is perfect for meal prepping. Leftovers can be refrigerated for up to 4 days or frozen for up to 3 months. Reheat gently in the microwave or on the stovetop.

SLOW COOKER
JAMBALAYA

ENJOY A DELICIOUS, BALANCED, AND SATISFYING MEAL WITH
MINIMAL EFFORT!

- THIS RECIPE IS VERSATILE AND CAN BE EASILY ADAPTED TO SUIT INDIVIDUAL TASTES OR DIETARY REQUIREMENTS.

- SLOW COOKING PRESERVES NUTRIENTS WHILE TENDERIZING TOUGHER CUTS OF MEAT, MAKING IT A HEALTHIER OPTION COMPARED TO OTHER COOKING METHODS.
SUBSTITUTING GREEK YOGURT FOR SOUR CREAM ADDS PROTEIN AND REDUCES FAT CONTENT.
USING WHOLE WHEAT PASTA OR GLUTEN-FREE NOODLES CAN ACCOMMODATE DIFFERENT DIETARY PREFERENCES WHILE ADDING FIBER OR MAKING IT GLUTEN-FREE.
ADDING SPINACH OR PEAS ENHANCES THE DISH'S NUTRITIONAL VALUE WITH EXTRA FIBER, VITAMINS, AND MINERALS.

BEEF STROGANOFF

6 PERSON   **6-8 HOURS**   **15 MINUTES**

INSTRUCTIONS

1. Optional (but recommended): Brown the beef: -Heat a large skillet over medium-high heat. Add olive oil, and brown the beef on all sides for about 2-3 minutes per side. This adds extra flavor but can be skipped if pressed for time.
2. Layer ingredients in the slow cooker: -Place the diced onions, minced garlic, and sliced mushrooms in the bottom of the slow cooker. Add the browned beef (or uncooked beef if skipping the browning step).
3. Prepare the sauce: In a small bowl, whisk together beef broth, Worcestershire sauce, Dijon mustard, tomato paste, paprika (if using), salt, and pepper. Pour this mixture over the beef and vegetables in the slow cooker.
4. Cook on low or high:
    Low setting: Cook for 6-8 hours.
    High setting: Cook for 4-5 hours.
    The beef should be tender, and the vegetables soft by the end of cooking.
5. Thicken the sauce: In the last 30 minutes of cooking, whisk the flour (or cornstarch) into the sour cream (or Greek yogurt). Stir the mixture into the slow cooker and let it cook for the remaining 30 minutes to thicken the sauce. (If adding spinach or peas, do so at this stage.)
6. Cook the noodles: Cook the egg noodles according to the package instructions if using them. Whole wheat or gluten-free pasta can be substituted for added nutrition or dietary needs.
7. Serve: Once the sauce has thickened, serve the Beef Stroganoff over the cooked egg noodles or pasta of choice. Alternatively, serve over mashed potatoes, rice, or even cauliflower mash for a low-carb option.

INGREDIENTS

1 ½ lbs (680g) beef stew meat (or lean beef chuck, cut into 1-inch cubes)
1 medium onion (diced)
3 cloves garlic (minced)
8 oz (227g) mushrooms (sliced; white button or cremini)
1 ½ cups (355ml) beef broth (low-sodium)
1 tbsp Worcestershire sauce
1 tbsp Dijon mustard
1 tbsp tomato paste
½ tsp paprika (optional)
Salt and pepper (to taste)
½ cup (120g) sour cream (use Greek yogurt as a healthier option)
2 tbsp all-purpose flour (or cornstarch for gluten-free)
2 tbsp olive oil (optional for browning meat)
12 oz (340g) egg noodles (optional, or use whole wheat pasta for added fiber)

OPTIONAL ADDITIONS:

1 cup baby spinach (added at the end for extra greens)
1 tsp dried thyme or parsley (for an herbal note)
½ cup peas (added in the last 30 minutes)

NUTRITIONAL

Calories: 375
Protein: 28g
Carbohydrates: 32g
Fat: 14g
Fiber: 3g
Cholesterol: 95mg
Sodium: 500mg
Potassium: 600mg

TOPPINGS OR GARNISHES

Chopped fresh parsley
A sprinkle of paprika
Grated Parmesan cheese

4 PERSON   **4 HOURS**   **15 MINUTES**

INSTRUCTIONS

1. Prepare the Slow Cooker: Lightly coat the inside of the slow cooker with olive oil or cooking spray to prevent sticking.

2. Add Ingredients: Place the baby red potatoes, corn, smoked sausage (if using), onion, garlic, Cajun seasoning, paprika, dried thyme, and cayenne pepper (if desired) into the slow cooker. Pour in the chicken broth, ensuring the ingredients are mostly submerged.

3. Cook: For high heat, cook on the high setting for 2 hours.
    For low heat, cook on the low setting for 4 hours, or until the potatoes are tender.

4. Add Shrimp and Lemon: Once the potatoes are tender, add the shrimp to the slow cooker, along with the lemon quarters. Stir gently to combine.

5. Continue Cooking: Cover and cook for an additional 15-20 minutes on high or until the shrimp are pink and opaque.

6. Adjust Seasoning: Taste and adjust the seasoning with salt, pepper, or additional Cajun seasoning, if needed.

7. Serve: Transfer the shrimp boil to serving bowls. Garnish with freshly chopped parsley. Optionally, serve with additional hot sauce or lemon wedges on the side.

INGREDIENTS

1 lb (450g) medium shrimp (peeled and deveined)
1 lb (450g) baby red potatoes, halved
3 ears of corn, cut into thirds
1 lb (450g) smoked sausage, sliced into 1/2-inch
pieces (optional for additional protein)
1 large yellow onion, diced
4 cloves garlic, minced
2 tbsp olive oil
4 cups low-sodium chicken broth
2 tbsp Cajun seasoning (adjust to taste)
1 tsp paprika
1 tsp dried thyme
1/2 tsp cayenne pepper (optional for extra spice)
1 lemon, quartered
Salt and pepper to taste
2 tbsp fresh parsley, chopped (for garnish)

OPTIONAL ADDITIONS

1 cup green beans (trimmed)
1 cup cherry tomatoes, halved
1/4 cup hot sauce (adjust to taste)

TOPPINGS & GARNISHES

Fresh parsley
Lemon wedges
Hot sauce
Melted butter (for drizzling)

NUTRITIONAL

Calories: 420
Protein: 30g
Carbohydrates: 30g
Fat: 17g
Fiber: 5g
Cholesterol: 210mg
Sodium: 860mg
Potassium: 880mg

Slow cooking helps retain nutrients in vegetables and proteins, making this Cajun Shrimp Boil both flavorful and nutritious. It's a versatile recipe that can be adapted for various dietary preferences, and the slow cooker method ensures minimal hands-on time, making it ideal for busy days or any meal of the day.

CAJUN SHRIMP
BOIL

CHOCOLATE LAVA CAKE

INSTRUCTIONS

8 PERSON **2-3 HOURS** **15 MINUTES**

1. Prepare the slow cooker: Lightly grease the inside of a 4- to 6-quart slow cooker with coconut oil or nonstick spray to prevent the cake from sticking.

2. Make the cake batter: In a medium mixing bowl, whisk together the dry ingredients: whole wheat flour, coconut sugar, cocoa powder, baking powder, and salt. In a separate bowl, combine the wet ingredients: almond milk, melted coconut oil, and vanilla extract.

3. Pour the wet ingredients into the dry ingredients and mix until just combined. Stir in the dark chocolate chips and optional additions (chia seeds, nuts, or spices).

4. Pour into the slow cooker: Spread the cake batter evenly across the bottom of the slow cooker.

5. Prepare the lava topping: In a small bowl, whisk together the cocoa powder and coconut sugar. Gradually pour the hot water (or coffee) over the cocoa-sugar mixture, stirring until dissolved. Carefully pour this mixture over the cake batter in the slow cooker. Do not stir; the liquid will form the "lava" as it cooks.

6. Cook the cake: Cover the slow cooker with the lid and cook on high for 2-3 hours or on low for 4-5 hours, or until the cake is set on top but gooey in the center. The cake will be firm around the edges and have a molten chocolate sauce underneath.

7. Serve: Once done, spoon portions of the cake onto plates, making sure to scoop from the bottom to get both cake and lava sauce.

INGREDIENTS

1 cup whole wheat flour (for added fiber and nutrients)
1/2 cup coconut sugar (or any unrefined sugar of choice)
1/4 cup unsweetened cocoa powder
1 tsp baking powder
1/4 tsp salt
1/2 cup unsweetened almond milk (or any plant-based milk of choice)
1/4 cup melted coconut oil (or butter)
1 tsp vanilla extract
1/4 cup dark chocolate chips (70% cocoa or higher for extra antioxidants)

FOR THE LAVA TOPPING:

1/4 cup unsweetened cocoa powder
1/2 cup coconut sugar (or any unrefined sugar of choice)
1 1/2 cups hot water or brewed coffee (coffee enhances the chocolate flavor)

OPTIONAL ADDITIONS

1 tbsp chia seeds (for extra fiber and omega-3s)
1/4 cup chopped walnuts or almonds (for added crunch and healthy fats)
1/4 tsp cinnamon or a pinch of cayenne for a spicy kick

NUTRITIONAL

Calories: 260
Protein: 4g
Carbohydrates: 38g
Fat: 11g
Fiber: 6g
Sugar: 22g
Cholesterol: 0mg (using plant-based ingredients)
Sodium: 125mg
Potassium: 250mg

TOPPINGS AND GARNISHES

Fresh berries (like raspberries or strawberries)
A dollop of Greek yogurt or coconut whipped cream
A sprinkle of chopped nuts or cacao nibs
A drizzle of almond butter or tahini for extra creaminess

ENJOY THIS RICH, NOURISHING, VER-SATILE CHOCOLATE LAVA CAKE FOR ANY MEAL OR OC-CASION!

THIS CAKE IS MADE WITH WHOLE WHEAT FLOUR, DARK CHOCOLATE, AND UN-REFINED COCONUT SUGAR, PROVIDING MORE FIBER, ANTIOXIDANTS, AND VITA-MINS COMPARED TO TRADITIONAL DESSERTS. OPTIONAL INGREDIENTS LIKE CHIA SEEDS AND NUTS CAN FURTHER BOOST THE NUTRIENT PROFILE WITH OMEGA-3 FATTY ACIDS, FIBER, AND HEALTHY FATS. THE SLOW COOKER METHOD ALLOWS FOR HANDS-FREE COOKING, MAKING IT CONVENIENT FOR BUSY SCHEDULES WHILE ALSO PRESERVING MORE NUTRIENTS BY USING LOWER COOKING TEM-PERATURES.

6 PERSON **2-3 HOURS** **15 MINUTES**

INSTRUCTIONS

1. Prepare the Apples: Peel, core, and slice the apples into medium-thick slices. Place them in a large bowl and toss with lemon juice to prevent browning.
   Add the maple syrup (or honey), cinnamon, nutmeg, vanilla extract, and cornstarch. Stir until the apples are evenly coated.

2. Layer in the Slow Cooker: Lightly grease the slow cooker with coconut oil or butter to prevent sticking.
   Spread the apple mixture evenly across the bottom of the slow cooker.

3. Prepare the Crisp Topping: In a separate bowl, combine oats, almond flour (or whole wheat flour), coconut sugar (or brown sugar), chopped nuts (if using), cinnamon, and salt.
   Pour in the melted coconut oil (or butter) and stir until the mixture is crumbly and well-mixed.

4. Top the Apples: Spread the crisp topping evenly over the apples, ensuring complete coverage for a perfect crunch.

5. Cook: Set your slow cooker on High and cook for 2.5 to 3 hours or on Low for 5 to 6 hours, until the apples are tender and the topping is golden and crisp.
   For an extra crisp top, remove the lid for the last 30 minutes of cooking to allow steam to escape.

6. Serve: Once done, scoop the warm apple crisp into bowls.

INGREDIENTS

For the Apple Filling:
6 medium apples (preferably a mix of Granny Smith and Honeycrisp), peeled, cored, and sliced
2 tbsp fresh lemon juice
¼ cup maple syrup or honey (for natural sweetness)
1 tsp ground cinnamon
¼ tsp ground nutmeg
1 tsp vanilla extract
2 tbsp cornstarch or arrowroot powder (for thickening)
For the Crisp Topping:
1 cup old-fashioned rolled oats
½ cup almond flour or whole wheat flour (for extra fiber and a gluten-free option)
⅓ cup chopped nuts (optional; walnuts or pecans for added crunch)
¼ cup coconut oil or unsalted butter, melted
⅓ cup coconut sugar or brown sugar
½ tsp ground cinnamon
¼ tsp salt

OPTIONAL ADDITIONS

2 tbsp chia seeds or ground flaxseeds (for added fiber and omega-3s)
⅓ cup raisins or dried cranberries
1 tbsp hemp seeds or sunflower seeds for added crunch and protein

TOPPINGS & GARNISHES

Greek yogurt or vanilla yogurt for added protein
A drizzle of almond or peanut butter for healthy fats
Coconut whipped cream for a dairy-free option
A sprinkle of extra cinnamon or a handful of fresh berries

NUTRITIONAL

Calories: 300 kcal
Protein: 3g
Carbohydrates: 50g
Sugars: 30g
Fiber: 6g
Fat: 12g
Saturated Fat: 6g
Cholesterol: 0mg
Sodium: 100mg
Potassium: 350mg

This Crock Pot Apple Crisp is perfect for any meal, from breakfast to dessert, thanks to the nutritious apples, whole grains, and healthy fats. Using a slow cooker ensures minimal hands-on time while enhancing the natural sweetness of the apples without the need for refined sugars. The mix of oats and nuts provides heart-healthy fiber and fats, while the optional seeds and fruits add a boost of vitamins and minerals, appealing to various dietary preferences, including gluten-free, dairy-free, and plant-based diets.

CROCK POT
APPLE CRISP

6 PERSON

4 HOURS

15 MINUTES

INSTRUCTIONS

1. Prepare the Peach Filling: In a large bowl, combine the sliced peaches, granulated sugar, lemon juice, vanilla extract, ground cinnamon, and optional nutmeg. Toss well to coat the peaches evenly. Sprinkle the cornstarch (or arrowroot powder) over the peach mixture and toss again until evenly distributed. This will help thicken the filling as it cooks.

2. Assemble the Peach Filling: Transfer the peach mixture into the slow cooker, spreading it out evenly.

3. Prepare the Cobbler Topping: In a medium bowl, whisk together the flour, granulated sugar, baking powder, baking soda, and salt. Cut the cold butter into the flour mixture using a pastry cutter or your fingers until the mixture resembles coarse crumbs. Stir in the buttermilk and vanilla extract until just combined. The batter will be lumpy; do not overmix.

4. Add the Cobbler Topping: Drop spoonfuls of the cobbler batter evenly over the peach filling in the slow cooker. The batter will spread out during cooking.

5. Cook the Cobbler: Cover the slow cooker with the lid.
   Set the slow cooker to low and cook for 4 hours, or on high for 2 hours, until the topping is golden brown and a toothpick inserted into the center of the topping comes out clean.

6. Serve: Let the cobbler cool for a few minutes before serving. This will allow the filling to set a bit.

INGREDIENTS

For the Peach Filling:
4 cups fresh or frozen peaches, peeled and sliced (about 1 lb or 450 g)
1/2 cup granulated sugar (can substitute with honey or maple syrup for a healthier option)
1 tablespoon lemon juice
1 teaspoon vanilla extract
1/4 teaspoon ground cinnamon
1/4 teaspoon ground nutmeg (optional)
2 tablespoons cornstarch or arrowroot powder (to thicken)
For the Cobbler Topping:
1 cup all-purpose flour (can substitute with whole wheat flour or a gluten-free blend)
1/4 cup granulated sugar
1/2 teaspoon baking powder
1/4 teaspoon baking soda
1/4 teaspoon salt
1/4 cup cold unsalted butter, cut into small pieces
1/2 cup buttermilk (or dairy-free milk for a vegan option)
1/2 teaspoon vanilla extract

OPTIONAL ADDITIONS

1/4 cup chopped nuts (e.g., pecans or walnuts) for added crunch
1/4 cup shredded coconut for extra flavor
1/2 teaspoon ground ginger for a spicier kick

TOPPINGS & GARNISHES

Serve the cobbler warm with a scoop of vanilla ice cream or a dollop of whipped cream for a classic touch.
Fresh mint leaves can add a refreshing contrast.
A sprinkle of granola can provide extra crunch and nutrition.

NUTRITIONAL

Calories: 320
Protein: 4 g
Carbohydrates: 48 g
Fat: 13 g
Fiber: 3 g
Cholesterol: 30 mg
Sodium: 220 mg
Potassium: 290 mg

Convenience: This slow cooker recipe requires minimal hands-on time, making it perfect for busy schedules.
Nutritional: Peaches are rich in vitamins A and C, antioxidants, and fiber. By adjusting the sugar and using whole grain or gluten-free flours, you can tailor the recipe to fit various dietary preferences.

PEACH COBBLER

ENJOY THIS DE-LICIOUS, EASY-TO-MAKE PEACH COBBLER AT ANY MEAL—WHETHER AS A COMFORT-ING DESSERT OR A SWEET BREAKFAST TREAT!

ENJOY THIS BREAD PUDDING FOR BREAKFAST, DESSERT, OR EVEN A LIGHT LUNCH, KNOWING IT'S PACKED WITH WHOLESOME INGREDIENTS!

SLOW COOKING ENHANCES FLAVOR WHILE PRESERVING NUTRIENTS, ESPECIALLY IN WHOLE GRAINS AND VEGETABLES. THIS BREAD PUDDING RECIPE CAN BE CUSTOMIZED FOR VARIOUS DIETARY PREFERENCES, USING PLANT-BASED MILK, WHOLE GRAIN BREAD FOR ADDED FIBER, AND OPTIONAL INGREDIENTS LIKE CHIA SEEDS AND FLAXSEED FOR A NUTRIENT BOOST. SLOW COOKERS ARE CONVENIENT AS THEY REQUIRE MINIMAL SUPERVISION, MAKING MEAL PREPARATION EASIER FOR BUSY DAYS.

BREAD PUDDING

6 PERSON   **2-2.5 HOURS**   **15 MINUTES**

INSTRUCTIONS

1. Prepare the Bread: Start by cutting the bread into cubes, about 1-inch in size. If using fresh bread, leave it out for a few hours to dry slightly, which helps it absorb the custard mixture better.

2. Mix the Wet Ingredients: In a large bowl, whisk together the eggs, almond milk, maple syrup, vanilla extract, cinnamon, nutmeg, and salt until well combined. You can substitute almond milk with any milk of your choice, such as oat, coconut, or dairy milk.

3. Add the Optional Ingredients: If you want to add more flavor or nutrition, stir in the chia seeds, raisins, chopped nuts, and any optional fruit, such as apple or mashed banana, into the wet mixture.

4. Combine Bread and Wet Mixture: Place the cubed bread into the slow cooker. Pour the egg mixture over the bread, making sure all the bread cubes are well-coated. Gently press the bread down with a spatula so that it soaks up the liquid evenly.

5. Set the Slow Cooker: Set the slow cooker to low heat. Cover and cook for 2 to 2.5 hours, or until the bread pudding is set and the top is golden. The cooking time may vary slightly depending on the model of your slow cooker, so check for doneness by inserting a knife into the center. If it comes out clean, the pudding is ready.

6. Serve Warm or Cold: Once the bread pudding is done, turn off the slow cooker and let it cool slightly before serving. You can enjoy it warm, or refrigerate it and serve cold later.

INGREDIENTS

6 cups cubed whole grain bread (preferably day-old or slightly stale)
4 large eggs
2 ½ cups unsweetened almond milk (or any milk of choice)
⅓ cup pure maple syrup (or honey for a sweeter version)
1 tsp vanilla extract
1 tsp ground cinnamon
¼ tsp ground nutmeg (optional for a warm, spiced flavor)
1 tbsp chia seeds (optional for added fiber and nutrition)
¼ cup raisins (optional for natural sweetness)
¼ cup chopped nuts (optional for crunch and healthy fats)
Pinch of salt

TOPPINGS OR GARNISHES

Fresh berries (strawberries, blueberries, raspberries)
A drizzle of maple syrup or honey
A dollop of Greek yogurt
Chopped nuts or seeds (e.g., almonds, walnuts, sunflower seeds)
A sprinkle of cinnamon or powdered sugar

NUTRITIONAL

Calories: 245
Protein: 8g
Carbohydrates: 39g
Fat: 6g
Fiber: 6g
Sugar: 12g
Cholesterol: 115mg
Sodium: 270mg
Potassium: 215mg

OPTIONAL ADDITIONS

1 medium apple (peeled, cored, and chopped)
1 ripe banana (mashed)
2 tbsp ground flaxseed (for added fiber)
¼ cup dark chocolate chips (for a dessert-like treat)
Potassium: 215mg

6 PERSON   **3-4 HOURS**   **10 MINUTES**

INSTRUCTIONS

1. Prepare the Slow Cooker: Lightly grease the sides of the slow cooker with a bit of coconut oil or butter to prevent the pudding from sticking.

2. Combine Ingredients: In the slow cooker, add the rice, almond milk, coconut milk, maple syrup (or honey), vanilla extract, cinnamon, nutmeg, and salt. Stir to combine the ingredients well.

3. Cook on High or Low: For faster cooking, set the slow cooker to high and cook for 3-4 hours, stirring occasionally. For a slower cook, set the slow cooker to low and cook for 6-8 hours, stirring every 2 hours.

4. Monitor the Rice: Around the 2-hour mark on high (or 4-hour mark on low), check the rice for doneness. If the rice is too thick, add more almond milk to reach your desired consistency.

5. Add Raisins (Optional): In the last 30 minutes of cooking, stir in raisins, cranberries, chia seeds, or flaxseeds if using. This adds extra nutrition and texture.

6. Check for Sweetness: Taste the pudding and adjust sweetness if needed by adding more maple syrup or honey.

7. Finish Cooking: Once the rice is soft and the mixture has thickened, turn off the slow cooker and let it sit uncovered for about 10 minutes to thicken further.

INGREDIENTS

1 cup white or brown rice (uncooked, preferably short grain)
4 cups unsweetened almond milk (or any milk of your choice)
½ cup coconut milk (for creaminess)
¼ cup maple syrup or honey (adjust to taste)
1 teaspoon vanilla extract
1 teaspoon ground cinnamon (optional)
¼ teaspoon ground nutmeg (optional)
¼ teaspoon salt
½ cup raisins or dried cranberries (optional)
1 tablespoon chia seeds (optional, for added fiber)
1 tablespoon flaxseeds (optional, for added nutrition)

TOPPINGS & GARNISHES

Fresh fruit: Sliced bananas, berries, or mango
Nuts: Almonds, pecans, or walnuts
Seeds: Sunflower seeds, hemp seeds
Drizzle of honey, maple syrup, or almond butter

NUTRITIONAL

Calories: 220 kcal
Protein: 4g
Carbohydrates: 36g
Fat: 7g
Fiber: 3g
Cholesterol: 0mg
Sodium: 130mg
Potassium: 200mg

This slow-cooked rice pudding is an easy, hands-off recipe that can be enjoyed warm or cold for breakfast, dessert, or a snack. Using almond and coconut milk makes it dairy-free and vegan, while chia and flaxseeds offer a nutrient boost with omega-3s and fiber.

RICE PUDDING

BUFFALO CHICKEN DIP

INSTRUCTIONS

8 PERSON   **2-3 HOURS**   **10 MINUTES**

1. Prepare the Slow Cooker: Lightly spray the inside of your slow cooker with cooking spray or line it with a slow cooker liner for easy cleanup.
2. Mix the Base: In a large mixing bowl, combine the softened cream cheese, Greek yogurt, buffalo sauce, and ranch dressing. Stir until smooth and well combined.
3. Add the Chicken and Cheese: Fold in the shredded chicken, shredded cheddar cheese, garlic powder, onion powder, smoked paprika (if using), and any optional additions like diced celery or bell pepper. Stir to distribute everything evenly.
4. Transfer to Slow Cooker: Pour the mixture into the prepared slow cooker and spread it out evenly.
5. Cook: Cover the slow cooker with the lid and set it to LOW. Cook for 2 to 3 hours, or until the dip is hot and bubbly. Stir occasionally if desired.
6. Check and Adjust: After about 2 hours, check the dip. If it's bubbling and the cheese is melted, it's ready. Season with additional salt and pepper if needed.
7. Serve: Once cooked, stir the dip one last time and garnish with fresh parsley or chives if desired.
8. Serving Suggestions: Serve warm with your choice of dippers: whole-grain crackers, sliced veggies (like carrots, cucumbers, or celery), or pita chips.

    For a heartier meal, spoon the dip onto baked sweet potatoes, lettuce wraps, or whole-grain toast.

INGREDIENTS

2 cups cooked, shredded chicken breast (about 2 large chicken breasts)
8 oz reduced-fat cream cheese (softened)
½ cup plain Greek yogurt (for extra protein)
½ cup buffalo sauce (adjust for spice preference; Frank's RedHot is a good option)
¼ cup ranch dressing (light or regular; can be substituted with blue cheese dressing)
1 cup shredded cheddar cheese (reduced-fat for a lighter option)
1 tsp garlic powder
1 tsp onion powder
½ tsp smoked paprika (optional for extra depth of flavor)
1 tbsp fresh lemon juice (optional for freshness)
Salt and pepper (to taste)
1 tbsp chopped fresh parsley or chives (optional for garnish)

TOPPINGS AND GARNISHES

Sliced green onions or fresh cilantro for a refreshing contrast.
Add a sprinkle of crumbled blue cheese for a more traditional buffalo chicken flavor.
Diced avocado for extra creaminess and healthy fats.

OPTIONAL ADDITIONS

½ cup diced celery (for added crunch and fiber)
½ cup diced red bell pepper (for color and extra nutrition)

NUTRITIONAL

Calories: 195
Protein: 17g
Carbohydrates: 5g
Fat: 12g
Fiber: 0.5g
Cholesterol: 60mg
Sodium: 600mg
Potassium: 210mg

THIS SLOW-COOKER BUFFALO CHICKEN DIP IS NOT ONLY INCRED-
IBLY EASY BUT ALSO A NUTRITIOUS WAY TO ENJOY A FLAVORFUL,
PROTEIN-PACKED MEAL WITH THE CONVENIENCE OF SLOW COOK-
ING. YOU CAN CUSTOMIZE IT FOR DIFFERENT DIETARY NEEDS, MAK-
ING IT A VERSATILE AND CROWD-PLEASING DISH.

8 PERSON   **2 HOURS**   **10 MINUTES**

INSTRUCTIONS

1. Prepare the ingredients: Thaw and drain the frozen spinach thoroughly, squeezing out excess water. Drain and chop the artichoke hearts into small pieces.

2. Mix the base: In a medium mixing bowl, combine the softened cream cheese, Greek yogurt, and garlic. Stir until smooth and well combined.

3. Add the remaining ingredients: Mix in the spinach, artichokes, mozzarella, Parmesan, and cheddar cheeses, along with the seasonings (black pepper, onion powder, dried basil, red pepper flakes, and salt). Stir until everything is well incorporated.

4. Transfer to the slow cooker: Lightly grease the slow cooker insert with cooking spray or olive oil to prevent sticking. Pour the spinach and artichoke mixture into the slow cooker and spread it out evenly.

5. Cook the dip: Set the slow cooker to high for 2 hours or low for 3–4 hours. Stir halfway through cooking to ensure even heat distribution. The dip should be warm, creamy, and the cheese fully melted by the end.

6. Optional topping ideas: Once the dip is done, you can sprinkle the top with extra Parmesan cheese, fresh chopped parsley, or even a drizzle of olive oil for added flavor.

7. Serve and enjoy: Serve the dip warm with whole-grain crackers, vegetable sticks (carrots, celery, cucumbers), or toasted pita chips for a nutritious option.

INGREDIENTS

10 oz frozen spinach, thawed and drained (about 1 cup, packed)
1 (14 oz) can of artichoke hearts, drained and chopped
8 oz low-fat cream cheese, softened
1/2 cup plain Greek yogurt (or sour cream)
1/2 cup shredded mozzarella cheese
1/4 cup grated Parmesan cheese
1/4 cup shredded part-skim cheddar cheese
2 cloves garlic, minced
1/4 tsp black pepper
1/2 tsp onion powder
1/2 tsp dried basil
1/4 tsp crushed red pepper flakes (optional for spice)
1/4 tsp salt (optional, adjust to taste)

OPTIONAL ADDITIONS

1/4 cup sun-dried tomatoes (for added sweetness and flavor)
2 tbsp flaxseeds or chia seeds (for extra fiber)
1 tbsp nutritional yeast (for a cheesy, vegan-friendly flavor)

TOPPINGS & GARNISHES

Fresh parsley or chives
Additional Parmesan cheese
Squeeze of lemon juice for brightness
Red pepper flakes for heat

NUTRITIONAL

Calories: 180
Protein: 8g
Carbohydrates: 6g
Fat: 14g
Saturated Fat: 7g
Fiber: 2g
Cholesterol: 35mg
Sodium: 430mg
Potassium: 200mg

Hands-off convenience: Slow cooking allows you to prep the ingredients, set the timer, and go about your day while the dish cooks itself.
Healthy cooking: Slow cooking preserves nutrients, especially in vegetables like spinach and artichokes, which are rich in vitamins A, C, and K.
Customizable: You can easily adjust this recipe to fit dietary preferences, such as making it vegan by using plant-based cream cheese and nutritional yeast instead of dairy-based cheeses.

SPINACH & ARTICHOKE DIP

ENJOY THIS NOURISHING, DELICIOUS, AND SIMPLE-TO-MAKE SPINACH & ARTI-CHOKE DIP ANY-TIME!

6 PERSON   **4-6 HOURS**   **15 MINUTES**

INSTRUCTIONS

1. Prepare the Meatballs: In a large mixing bowl, combine the ground meat, breadcrumbs, Parmesan cheese (if using), milk, egg, onion, garlic, parsley, oregano, salt, pepper, and red pepper flakes (if desired). Mix well until all ingredients are fully incorporated.

2. Form the Meatballs: Using your hands or a small ice cream scoop, form the mixture into 1-1.5 inch meatballs. You should have about 18-20 meatballs.

3. Optional Browning (for added flavor): Heat 1 tbsp of olive oil in a skillet over medium heat. Brown the meatballs in batches, turning them occasionally until they are lightly browned on all sides. This step is optional but adds more flavor to the dish.

4. Slow Cooker Setup: Place the meatballs in the Crock Pot. Pour the marinara sauce over the meatballs, ensuring they are mostly covered by the sauce. If you're using a larger slow cooker, you can layer the meatballs and sauce.

5. Cook the Meatballs:
   Low Setting: Cook on low for 4-6 hours.
   High Setting: Cook on high for 2-3 hours. The meatballs are done when they reach an internal temperature of 165°F (74°C) and are tender.

6. Serve: Gently stir the meatballs and sauce before serving. You can serve them over pasta, rice, mashed potatoes, or zucchini noodles for a lower-carb option.

INGREDIENTS

1 lb (450g) ground beef (or ground turkey for a leaner option)
1/2 cup breadcrumbs (use whole wheat for added fiber)
1/4 cup grated Parmesan cheese (optional, omit for dairy-free)
1/4 cup milk (use almond or oat milk for dairy-free)
1 large egg
1 small onion, finely chopped
2 garlic cloves, minced
1 tbsp fresh parsley, chopped (or 1 tsp dried parsley)
1 tsp dried oregano
1/2 tsp salt (reduce for low-sodium diets)
1/4 tsp black pepper
1/4 tsp red pepper flakes (optional for a kick)
2 cups marinara sauce (homemade or store-bought, low-sodium recommended)
1 tbsp olive oil (optional for browning)

OPTIONAL ADDITIONS

1/2 tsp smoked paprika for a smoky flavor
1 tbsp Worcestershire sauce for a deeper, umami taste
1/4 cup finely grated carrots or zucchini for added nutrition

TOPPINGS & GARNISHES

Freshly chopped basil or parsley
Grated Parmesan cheese (optional)
Red pepper flakes for extra heat

NUTRITIONAL

Calories: 310 kcal
Protein: 22g
Carbohydrates: 16g
Fat: 18g
Fiber: 2g
Cholesterol: 105mg
Sodium: 560mg
Potassium: 600mg

Slow cooking retains nutrients from ingredients, especially vegetables, while reducing the need for excessive oil or frying.
Ground turkey can be used for a leaner option with less saturated fat.
Low-sodium marinara sauce makes the dish heart-healthy, while adding vegetables like zucchini or carrots increases the fiber and vitamin content.

CROCK POT
MEATBALLS

● ENJOY THESE NU-
TRITIOUS AND
VERSATILE MEAT-
BALLS FOR ANY
MEAL OF THE DAY!

ENJOY THIS EASY
AND NOURISHING
NACHO CHEESE
DIP AT ANY MEAL
OR AS A PARTY
SNACK!

NUTRITIONAL BALANCE: THIS DIP INCLUDES CHEESE, WHICH PROVIDES CALCI-UM AND PROTEIN, WHILE OPTIONAL ADDITIONS LIKE BEANS AND CORN BOOST FIBER AND NUTRIENTS.
SLOW COOKING: THE SLOW COOKER ALLOWS FOR HANDS-OFF PREPARATION, PERFECT FOR BUSY SCHEDULES. IT ALSO MELDS FLAVORS BEAUTIFULLY, MAK-ING THE DIP RICHER AND MORE FLAVORFUL.
VERSATILE: THIS RECIPE CAN BE ADAPTED TO SUIT VARIOUS DIETARY PREFER-ENCES, INCLUDING DAIRY-FREE AND LIGHTER OPTIONS, WHILE MAINTAINING GREAT TASTE AND TEXTURE.

NACHO CHEESE DIP

8 PERSON

2 HOURS

15 MINUTES

INSTRUCTIONS

1. Prepare the Slow Cooker:
   Set your slow cooker to "low" or "high" depending on how quickly you want to make the dip.
2. Combine Ingredients:
   In a large mixing bowl, combine the shredded cheddar cheese, Monterey Jack cheese, condensed cheddar cheese soup, milk, sour cream (or Greek yogurt), diced tomatoes, diced green chilies, and chopped onions. Mix well.
3. Season and Adjust Consistency:
   Stir in the taco seasoning. If you prefer a thicker dip, dissolve the cornstarch in a small amount of cold milk and add it to the mixture. Stir well to combine. Season with salt and pepper to taste.
4. Transfer to Slow Cooker:
   Pour the cheese mixture into the slow cooker. If using optional ingredients like black beans, corn, jalapeños, or bell peppers, stir them in now.
5. Cook the Dip:
   Cover and cook on "low" for 4 hours or "high" for 2 hours, stirring occasionally. The dip is done when the cheese is fully melted and all ingredients are well blended.
6. Final Stir and Serve:
   Stir the dip thoroughly before serving to ensure even consistency. Adjust seasoning if necessary.

INGREDIENTS

2 cups shredded sharp cheddar cheese
1 cup shredded Monterey Jack cheese
1 can (10.5 oz) condensed cheddar cheese soup
1 cup milk (or a dairy-free alternative)
1/2 cup sour cream (or Greek yogurt for a lighter option)
1/2 cup diced tomatoes (canned, drained)
1/2 cup diced green chilies (canned, drained)
1/2 cup finely chopped onions
1 tablespoon taco seasoning (or to taste)
1 tablespoon cornstarch (optional, for thickening)
Salt and pepper to taste

TOPPINGS OR GARNISHES

Chopped fresh cilantro
Sliced green onions
Diced tomatoes
Sour cream or Greek yogurt
Sliced black olives
Crushed tortilla chips
Sliced avocado or guacamole

NUTRITIONAL

Calories: 260
Protein: 12g
Carbohydrates: 18g
Fat: 18g
Fiber: 2g
Cholesterol: 50mg
Sodium: 750mg
Potassium: 350mg

OPTIONAL ADDITIONS

1/2 cup black beans (cooked and drained)
1/2 cup corn kernels (cooked)
1/2 cup sliced jalapeños (fresh or pickled)
1/2 cup diced bell peppers (any color)

10 PERSON   **2-3 HOURS**   **10 MINUTES**

INSTRUCTIONS

1. Prepare the ingredients:
    In a large mixing bowl, combine the Rice Chex, Whole Wheat Chex, pretzel twists, almonds, and pumpkin seeds.

2. Season the mix:
    In a small bowl, whisk together the olive oil, soy sauce (or tamari), garlic powder, onion powder, smoked paprika (if using), and black pepper. Pour this seasoning mixture over the dry ingredients and gently toss to coat everything evenly.

3. Transfer to the slow cooker:
    Lightly coat the inside of your slow cooker with a small amount of olive oil or non-stick spray to prevent sticking. Add the seasoned Chex mix into the slow cooker.

4. Slow cook:
    Set the slow cooker on low heat and cook for 2 hours, stirring every 30 minutes to prevent burning and ensure even toasting. After 2 hours, if the mix still feels slightly soft, cook for an additional 30 minutes uncovered to let any excess moisture evaporate.

5. Cool and store:
    Once done, transfer the Chex mix to a baking sheet or large tray to cool completely. If you plan to add dried cranberries or raisins, mix them in now. Store in an airtight container for up to 1 week.

INGREDIENTS

4 cups Rice Chex cereal
4 cups Whole Wheat Chex cereal
2 cups pretzel twists (preferably whole grain or gluten-free)
1 cup raw almonds (or other nuts like cashews or walnuts)
½ cup raw pumpkin seeds (pepitas) or sunflower seeds
2 tablespoons olive oil (or coconut oil for a richer flavor)
3 tablespoons low-sodium soy sauce or tamari (for gluten-free)
1 teaspoon garlic powder
1 teaspoon onion powder
½ teaspoon smoked paprika (optional for a smoky flavor)
¼ teaspoon black pepper

OPTIONAL ADDITIONS

1 tablespoon nutritional yeast for a cheesy flavor
½ teaspoon cayenne pepper for some heat
¼ cup dried cranberries or raisins for a touch of sweetness (added after cooking)

TOPPINGS & GARNISHES

Sprinkle with fresh herbs like parsley or cilantro before serving.
Top with a light drizzle of tahini or almond butter for a creamy touch.
For a sweet-salty version, sprinkle with a pinch of cinnamon and a drizzle of maple syrup before serving.

NUTRITIONAL

Calories: 190
Protein: 5g
Carbohydrates: 30g
Fiber: 4g
Sugars: 2g (without dried fruit)
Fat: 8g
Saturated Fat: 1g
Cholesterol: 0mg
Sodium: 240mg (using low-sodium soy sauce)
Potassium: 180mg

Using a slow cooker for this Chex mix helps preserve the nutritional quality of whole grains, nuts, and seeds. This method requires minimal oil, keeping the recipe low in unhealthy fats while allowing for customization to suit various dietary preferences (gluten-free, vegan, or nut-free).

SLOW COOKER
CHEX MIX

THIS SLOW-COOKER CHEX MIX IS A HEALTHIER TWIST ON THE TRADITIONAL SNACK. IT'S MADE WITH WHOLE GRAINS, NUTS, SEEDS, AND A TOUCH OF SEASONING. IT'S GREAT AS A SNACK OR WITH SALADS AND SOUPS FOR ANY MEAL. THE SLOW COOKER METHOD ENSURES THE MIX IS EVENLY TOASTED AND PACKED WITH FLAVOR WHILE PRESERVING NUTRIENTS.

ESSENTIAL TIPS FOR OPTIMAL USE

Setup and Initial Use

Before you start cooking with your Crock Pot, there are a few essential steps to take to ensure it's ready for use:

1. Washing: First, wash the removable insert (ceramic pot) and lid with warm, soapy water to remove any residue from packaging or manufacturing. Dry both components thoroughly before reassembling.

2. Handling Safely: Always ensure the Crock Pot is placed on a flat, heat-resistant surface, away from walls or other appliances. The exterior can warm during use, so provide sufficient clearance to avoid heat damage.

3. Preheating (optional): While not required for every recipe, preheating the Crock Pot for 10-15 minutes before adding ingredients can speed up the cooking process and help maintain consistent temperatures.

Properly setting up your Crock Pot will prevent early mishaps and ensure smooth operation from the start.

Efficient Operation

To maximize the efficiency of your Crock Pot and make the most of your time and energy:

1. Layering Ingredients: Place denser, slow-cooking ingredients like root vegetables and meats at the bottom of the pot and lighter, faster-cooking ingredients like greens or dairy-based sauces on top. This ensures even cooking and prevents burning.

2. Optimal Fill Level: Avoid overfilling the Crock Pot. Aim for it to be about half to two-thirds full. Overfilling can lead to uneven cooking, while underfilling can cause the dish to cook too quickly.

3. Use the Right Setting: Select the appropriate heat setting (low or high) based on your time. The low setting is ideal for longer cooking times (6-8 hours), while the high setting will cook dishes faster (4-6 hours). Use the **warm** setting after the dish is done to keep food ready to serve without overcooking.

4. Batch Cooking: When possible, cook larger portions and freeze leftovers. This way, you maximize the energy and time spent on each dish.

Advanced Techniques

To truly master the Crock Pot and take your cooking skills to the next level, consider these expert tips:

Expert Cooking Tips

1. Sear Meats for Better Flavor: Before adding meats to the Crock Pot, consider browning them in a skillet. This adds a deeper flavor through caramelization and enhances the dish's overall taste. Browning isn't required but can elevate simple recipes like pot roast, stew, or chili.

2. Deglazing the Pan: After browning meats, use a liquid like broth, wine, or water to deglaze the pan. Pour the liquid into the Crock Pot to capture all the browned bits stuck to the bottom of the pan, intensifying your dish's flavor.

3. Layer Herbs and Aromatics: Fresh herbs like rosemary, thyme, or bay leaves work best when layered on the ingredients. This allows the steam to circulate the aroma throughout the dish. Dried herbs can be added directly to the sauce or liquid for a more intense flavor.

4. Timing Dairy Additions: Dairy products like milk, cream, or cheese tend to curdle or separate during slow cooking. To avoid texture issues, add these ingredients during the last 30-60 minutes of cooking.

Mastering the Crock Pot

CREATIVE USES

The Crock-Pot is not just for traditional stews and roasts. With some creativity, you can use it for non-traditional recipes and tasks.

Beyond the Basics

1. Desserts: Try making desserts like "bread pudding", "fruit cobblers", or even a "molten chocolate lava cake" in your Crock Pot. The low, steady heat ensures even cooking without burning the delicate ingredients.
2. Yogurt Making: You can use the Crock Pot to make homemade yogurt by gently heating milk and then maintaining a low temperature for several hours as the cultures develop. This is a great way to save money and enjoy a healthier version of store-bought yogurt.
3. Candles and Soap: For DIY enthusiasts, the Crock Pot can melt wax for homemade candles or soap. Set it to low heat and monitor the temperature carefully.

ADAPTING TRADITIONAL RECIPES

You don't need to rely solely on Crock Pot-specific recipes to use the appliance. Many stovetop or oven recipes can be adapted:

1. Reduce Liquid: Slow cooking retains moisture, so reduce the amount of liquid in traditional recipes by about 20%. This ensures the dish doesn't become too watery.
2. Cooking Time Conversion: As a general rule of thumb, a recipe that takes 30 minutes to cook on the stovetop will require about 4-6 hours on "ow" or 2-3 hours on "high" in a Crock Pot.
3. Seasoning Adjustments: Strong flavors can mellow over long cooking periods. Taste and adjust seasoning toward the end of the cooking process to ensure balanced flavors.

Troubleshooting Common Problems

While the Crock Pot is simple to use, common issues may arise. Here are practical solutions to address them:

Common Issues and Fixes

1. Problem: Food is Undercooked

   Fix: Ensure the lid is kept on during cooking (every time you lift it, you lose heat). Check if the pot was overfilled, which could prevent food from cooking properly. Increase cooking time or switch to the high setting.
2. Problem: Food is Overcooked or Dry

   - Fix: This usually occurs when using the wrong setting or leaving the dish on too long. To avoid this, use the **warm** setting once the food is cooked, or set a timer to avoid overcooking.
3. Problem: Watery Dishes

   - Fix: Slow cookers retain liquid, so reduce the liquid in recipes by 20-25%. If your dish is still too watery, remove the lid during the last 30 minutes to let excess moisture evaporate.
4. Problem: Crock Pot Not Heating Properly

   - Fix: Ensure it's properly plugged in and the dial is set to the correct setting. If the problem persists, it may be a mechanical issue.

When to Contact Support

If you encounter any of the following issues, it's best to contact the manufacturer or seek professional help:

- The Crock-Pot isn't heating up despite being plugged in.
- The control panel or timer malfunctions.
- The ceramic insert develops cracks, or the lid doesn't fit properly.
- Any exposed wires or overheating of the exterior casing.

The Crock Pot is an invaluable tool that can transform your cooking routine, making meal prep easier and more enjoyable. Following these tips and tricks, you can master the Crock Pot, from efficient operation and advanced cooking techniques to troubleshooting common issues. With some experimentation and creativity, you'll discover that the Crock Pot can do more than slow-cook basic stews and roasts. Whether you're adapting your favorite recipes or exploring new uses like dessert-making or DIY projects, using your Crock Pot to its full potential can open up new culinary possibilities.

SIMPLE CROCKPOT

1500+ Days of Easy, Healthy, and Delicious
Slow Cook Meals to Elevate Your Cooking
with Minimal Effort

Made in the USA
Monee, IL
09 December 2024

72926741R00057